Wonders of Learning

BIG WORKBOOK

Year One

What every Year One child needs to know!

© 2022 North Parade Publishing

Editorial team: Jennifer G. Bove, Kris Anah Allard, Joel Riemer

UK editor: J. Emmerson-Hicks

Educational consultant: Susan Flavell

Published by North Parade Publishing, 3-6 Henrietta Mews, Bath BA2 6LR, United Kingdom

Printed in China, Guangdong Province 2022

First Printing

24 23 22 21 20 1 2 3 4 5

Contents

Dear Family,

What does it mean when we say that *Wonders of Learning* workbooks have been crafted with your child in mind?

Of course, we have not met your child. But we understand the uniqueness of each child's learning path, as well as the developmental stages that children have in common. Each page is designed to facilitate effective and enjoyable learning, either as a supplement to school-based learning or as part of a home-based course of study. Classic "pencil-and-paper" activities are complemented by pages that provide hands-on and enquiry-based learning opportunities.

Because children learn at different rates, pages are designed so that some children may complete them on their own while others may need more help from you. In the earliest years, your child will need you to read instructions aloud.

You are your child's first teacher and, whether your child attends school or studies at home, you will always be an important teacher. The earliest learning happens naturally and through repetition. Children learn about words and concepts each time you call something by its name – the difference between a cat and a dog, for example. They learn to count each time you use numbers to describe objects or events in everyday life. And many children learn to read by unconsciously memorising picture books that are read to them frequently.

Have fun working through this book with your child. Encourage curiosity as you explore new concepts and practice familiar ones. And throughout daily life, read to your child as often as possible, name and count what you see, and keep answering children's questions!

We have put our hearts into providing a resource that will be meaningful and memorable for your child, and we hope that you enjoy the results.

Yours sincerely,

The publishers

Phonics

the alphabet

Trace each upper case letter, and circle the matching lower case letter.

f a e

b s d

a c s

b d r

a e y

f p r

g q w

d h y

a e i

b j p

j k x

c j l

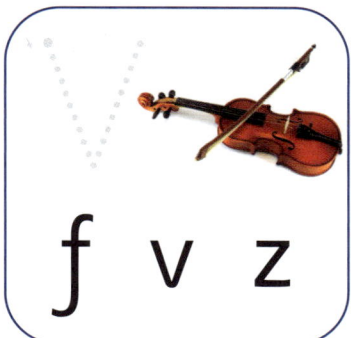

m   s   v

h   n   t

b   o   u

j   k   p

q   t   y

c   o   r

o   p   s

d   n   t

h   u   v

f   v   z

c   i   w

d   m   x

i   r   y

g   n   z

Did you know?
No two zebras have the same stripes! They are unique – just like our fingerprints.

the alphabet

Help the space rocket find its way home by filling in the missing letters in the correct order.

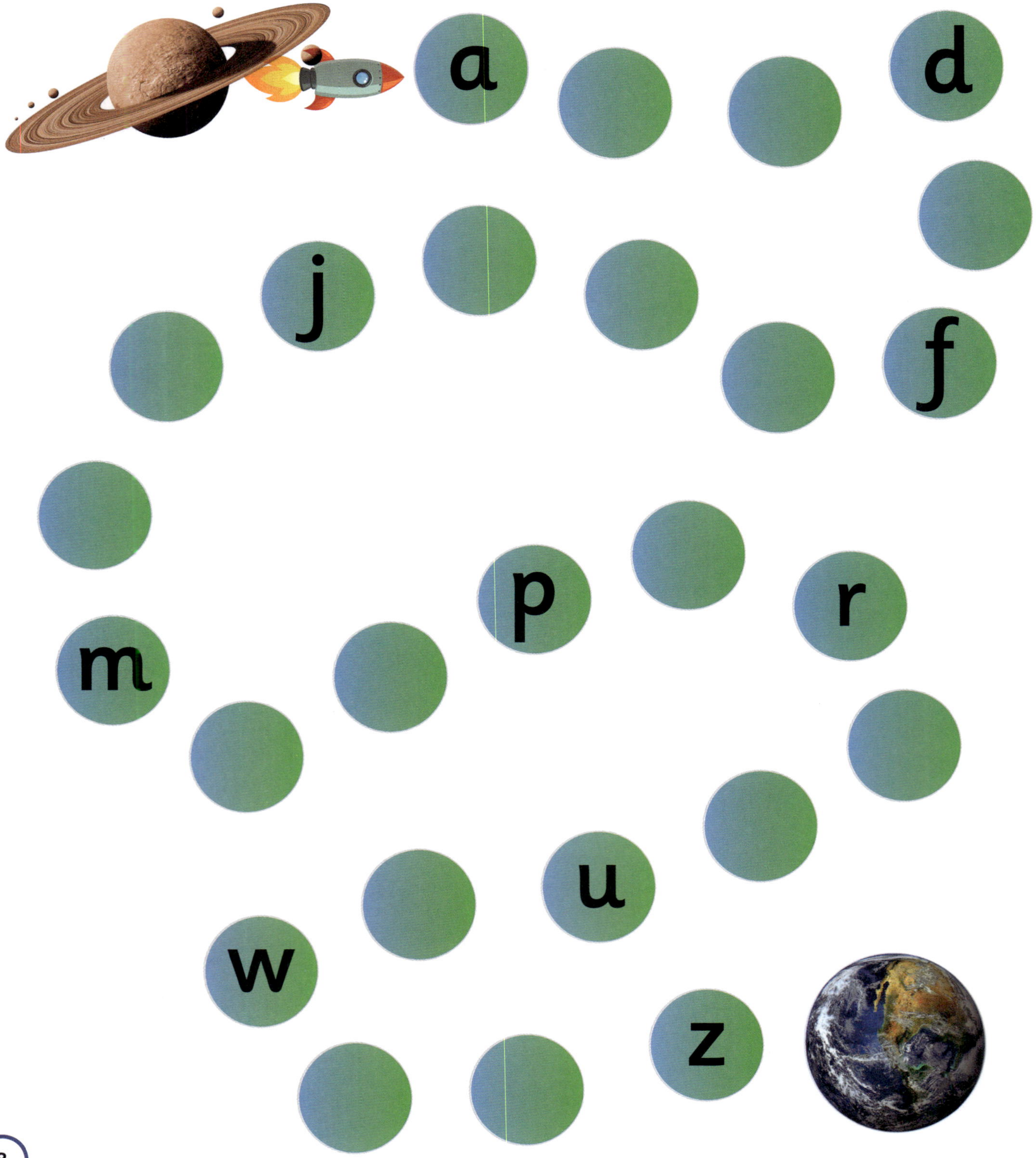

a   d

j

f

m   p   r

u

w

z

changes

Change one sound each time to create the next word.

hat	_at	ca_	_ap	m_p
				_op
b_t	ba_	_ag	ta_	t_p
oat				
c_t	_ot	h_t	_oot	b_t
				bea_
sh_p	_ip	chi_	_in	b_n

consonant blends

Complete the words by filling in the correct consonant blend.

lb	nd	mp	lk	ft
lt	st	nt	nch	

mi

gi

ne

te

be

la

bu

sa

be

| tw | fr | tr | scr | gr | fl |
| cr | sn | str | gr | st | br |

ab

ee

ins

ush

og

ar

ass

ag

ew

ing

ass

ail

vowels and consonants

! Each letter in the alphabet is a **vowel** or a **consonant**. Vowels make open sounds. That means that you can make the sound without parts of your mouth touching.

Say each letter sound below. Circle the letter if you can make the sound without closing any part of your mouth or throat.

a	e	i	o	u
b	k	l	p	m

You probably circled all the vowels … and none of the consonants!

! The letter **y** can act as both **vowel** and **consonant**.
Say '**yo-yo**'. The **y** sound is a *consonant* sound.
Say '**funny**'. The **y** sound is a *vowel* sound.

Look at each instance of the letter **y** in the poem below. If it makes a **vowel** sound, **circle** it. If it makes a **consonant** sound, draw a **line** under it.

Yellow birds
fly by in the sky,
Then land on the back
of a **y**ak – oh my!

vowel sounds

ay as in **day**

ie as in **pie**

ou as in **mountain**

Join the pictures to the right sounds.

The Wheels on the Bus

The wheels on the bus go round and round,
Round and round, round and round.
The wheels on the bus go round and round,
All day long!

clouds

sprouts

ay

ou

ie

fried

stingray

crayons

tie

vowel sounds

ea as in **treat**

ir as in **girl**

oy as in **joy**

Join the pictures to the right sounds.

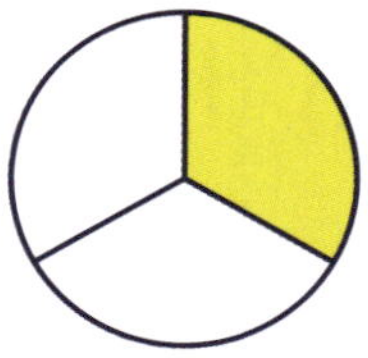

jeans

meat

bird

third

ea   **oy**

ir

oyster

boy

t-shirt

toys

beans

vowel sounds

ew as in **dew**

aw as in **drawer**

ue as in **queue**

Join the pictures to the right sounds.

paw

glue

nephew

aw   **ew**

ue

claw

tissues

screw

blue

saw

vowel sounds

oe as in doe

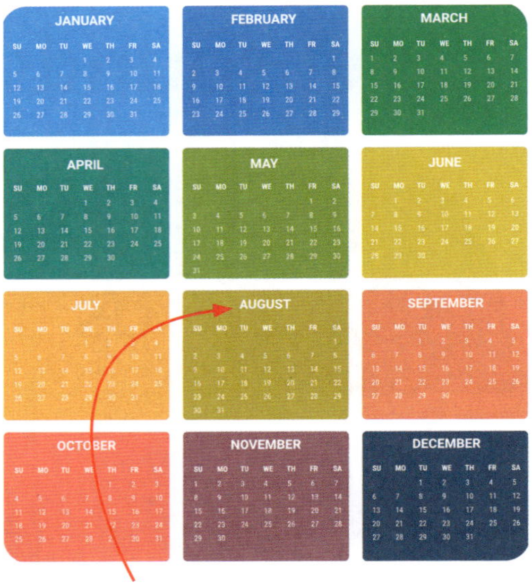

ey as in donkey

au as in August

Complete the words below by filling in the correct vowel sound. Then colour the images.

h __ nt

monk __

potat __ s

3 in a row

Take it in turns to read out one of the words on the grid. If you read it correctly, colour it in. Then the next player takes a turn, using a different colour. The first person to get three in a row is the winner.

enjoy	crayon	haunt	doe	treat	blue
claw	girl	sprout	yawn	bird	haul
launch	pie	glue	heat	dew	meat
toes	flew	paw	tray	cried	skirt
pray	shout	tie	toys	statue	about

same sound, different spelling

windmills

wheel

All these question words begin with **wh**.

why ? **what ?** **where**
? **when ?** **which ?**

Complete the words.

wh + eat = _____

wh + isk = _____

wh + ite = _____

wh + ale = _____

same sound, different spelling

food

photo

Circle the words that are **not** spelt with **ph**.

phone

fish

trophy

family

ABC
alphabet

nephew

fan

elephant

dolphin

microphone

split digraphs a—e

! When a '**magic e**' at the end of a word reaches back and changes the sound of the vowel before the consonant, it is known as a **split digraph**.

Trace and complete the words using the **magic e**.

cap ➡ cap_

tap ➡ tap_

 man ➡ man_

can ➡ can_

 mat ➡ mat_

The **magic e** changes the vowel sound from short to long!

Complete the words using the **a—e** digraph.

f l [ ] m   p l [ ] n   s k [ ] t

p l [ ] t   s n [ ] k   s p [ ] d

Draw lines to match the rhyming words.

pancake	game
shape	chase
stale	shade
fade	mistake
frame	grape
grade	kale
base	made

split digraphs e—e

Complete the words using the **e—e** digraph.

s w [ ] d [ ]

[ ] v [ ] n [ ]

t h [ ] s [ ]

c o m p l [ ] t [ ]

C h i n [ ] e [ ]

t h [ ] m [ ] p a r k

Did you know?
Rides similar to roller coasters were invented hundreds of years ago. Today, some roller coasters hit top speeds of more than 100 miles an hour!

split digraphs i—e

Complete the words using the **i—e** digraph.

| b | | k | | | s | t | r | | p | | s | | k | t | |

| h | | d | | w | h | | t | | s | m | | l | |

| c | h | | m | | s | l | | d | | l | | m | |

Did you know?
Limes and lemons are both citrus fruits. So are oranges and grapefruits. Citrus fruits have plenty of vitamin C to help you stay healthy!

split digraphs o—e

Complete the words using the **o—e** digraph.

r		p	

p	h		n	

r		s	

h		m	

g	l		b	

c		n	

Draw lines to match the rhyming words.

bone

hose

hope

broke

wrote

stole

nose

note

hole

stone

slope

poke

split digraphs u—e

Trace and complete the words using the **magic e**.

cub → cub_

tub → tub_

cut → cut_

Complete the words using the **u—e** digraph.

| r | | l | |

| c | o | s | t | m | |

| t | | n | |

Hap - py birth - day to you!

Did you know?
According to the Guinness Book of World Records, "Happy Birthday to You" is the most recognised song in the English language.

real and nonsense words

Read out loud the split digraph words below.
In each frame circle the words that are not real.

shape

brake

pale

place

wase

prale

save

blade

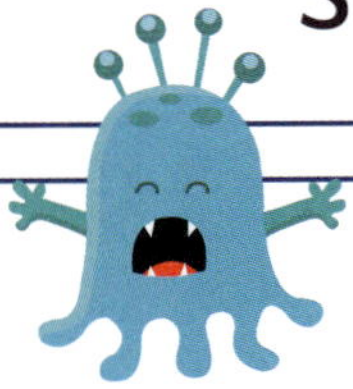

eken

prile

crocodile

spike

ride

time

libe

evening

spoke

throne

fode

dome

frozen

rode

bose

vote

duke

dune

dispute

crume

flute

perfume

stuse

excuse

split digraph game

Find a dice and two counters. Put your counters on the green square. Take turns with a friend to roll the dice and follow the code below. Identify the sound, and move your counter clockwise to the next square with a picture with that sound. If there isn't a square in front of you with that sound, skip the turn. The first one to reach the red square is the winner!

START →

Delete

FINISH

- a—e sound
- e—e sound
- i—e sound
- o—e sound
- u—e sound
- *not* a split digraph!

2 x 4 6 8

tricky words

Read the following words out loud, then practice writing them.

looked   looked   their   their

called   called   Mr   Mr

asked   asked   Mrs   Mrs

could   could   oh   oh

people   people

Now see if you can spot all the tricky words in the grid.
Circle each word when you find it.

y	c	b	f	M	r	s	r
l	o	c	a	l	l	e	d
o	u	a	M	s	i	y	s
o	l	s	p	t	o	h	l
k	d	k	t	h	e	i	r
e	v	e	w	s	M	w	o
d	b	d	M	u	r	b	o
x	p	e	o	p	l	e	p

same grapheme, different sound – i

In the following words the **i** makes a **short** vowel sound.

wig

pin

fin

Did you know?
Orcas are the largest species of dolphin. When it is healthy, its dorsal fin stands up. If the fin flops over, the animal may be sick or stressed.

But in some words the **i** makes a **long** vowel sound.

child

pint

kind

In the words below, does the **i** make a **long**, or **short** vowel sound? Draw a line to match up.

behind		fish
	long	
chin		wild
mind		stick
	short	
pillow		blind

same grapheme, different sound – o

hot

mother

cold

Circle the pictures with the **o** as in *hot* in green, those with the **o** as in *mother* in purple, and those with the **o** as in *cold* in orange.

comb

honey

dotty

love

old

monkey

bowls

frog

clock

Did you know?
Not all frogs are green. They come in many different colours.

same grapheme, different sound – u

run

push*

music

Draw a line to match the words below to the correct vowel sound.

unicorn

pull

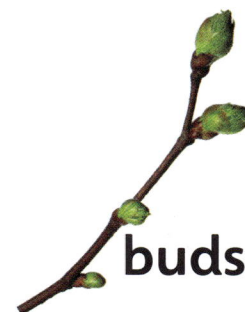
jug

cushion

u
as in **run**

u
as in **push**

buds

u
as in **music**

full

cup

duck

bull

human

tulip

uniform

❗ *In some regional pronunciations the vowel sound may be different.*

same grapheme, different sound – a

hat   **wasp**   **bath***   **baby**

Draw a line to match the words below to the correct vowel sound.

wash

fast

mask

watch

| a
as in **hat** | a
as in **wasp** |
| a
as in **bath** | a
as in **baby** |

lady

want

acorn

mat

apron   **grass**   **apple**

❗ In some regions the **a** in **bath** is pronounced the same as in **hat**.

same grapheme, different sound – ow

cow

crow

Sometimes a word can mean different things depending on how it is pronounced.

row *as in argument*

row *as in paddle*

Draw a line to match the words below to the correct vowel sound.

flower

ow
as in **cow**

ow
as in **crow**

snowman

sparrow

towel

frown

yellow

clown

grow

same grapheme, different sound – ou

We have looked at **ou** as in **mountain***.
Here are some other ways it can be pronounced.

group   **should**   **shoulder**

Practise saying and writing the words below.

group	you	soup
group	you	soup

should	would	could
should	would	could

shoulder	mouldy	boulder
shoulder	mouldy	boulder

*page 13

same grapheme, different sound – ie

pie*

thief

Cut out the words on page 353 and glue them in the correct box.

ie as in **pie**	*ie* as in **thief**

same grapheme, different sound – ea

treat*

bread

Circle the pictures with the **ea** as in *treat* in red, and those with the **ea** as in *bread* in blue.

treasure

peas

eagle

meal

weather

feather

leaf

easel

breakfast

measure

*page 15

same grapheme, different sound – or

torn

work

Draw a line to match the words below to the correct vowel sound.

torch

horn

fast happy
house
pencil music

words

| **or** as in **torn** | **or** as in **work** |

horse

fork

0 / 10
worst

corn

worm

world

same grapheme, different sound – ey

monkey

prey

Draw a line to match the words below to the correct vowel sound.

honey

key

trolley

ey
as in **prey**

survey

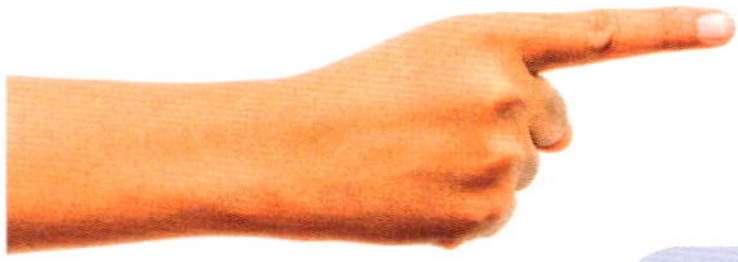

obey

ey
as in **monkey**

grey

osprey

turkey

money

same grapheme, different sound – y

The letter **y** has several different sounds.

yo-yo

consonant sound
at start of word or syllable

try

long i sound
at end of single syllable word

rhythm

short i sound
between consonants

funny

ee sound
at end of two syllable word

Draw lines from the pictures to link them to the matching **y** sound.

penny

sky

yolk

bicycle

! See page 13 for how **y** sounds in the **ay** digraph.

same grapheme, different sound – g

goat
hard sound

gentle
soft sound

Draw a line to match the words below to the correct vowel sound.

gorilla

games

gems

soft g

hard g

gymnastics

giraffe

orange

gum

bug

same grapheme, different sound – c

cat

hard sound

cereal

soft sound

Circle the pictures with the **hard** sound in green, and those with the **soft** sound in purple.

cycle

icy

cylinder

caterpillar

crown

calendar

centre

cent

carton

calm

Did you know?
There are 365 days in a normal calendar year, but it actually takes the Earth about 365 days, 5 hours and 49 minutes to go around the Sun once. This is why we have leap years!

same grapheme, different sound – ch

cherries   Christmas   chef

Practise saying and writing the words below.

teacher  cheese   reach

teacher   cheese   reach

scheme   chord 🎄 ache

scheme   chord   ache

chute 👨‍🍳 machine   chalet

chute   machine   chalet

missing words

Read the sentences. Fill in the correct missing word from the three choices.

Paul likes to _____ his bicycle in the lane.

eat / bake / ride

Eve bakes tasty cupcakes with her _____.

drawer / mother / clown

A bowl of _____ is a good way to start the day.

cereal / singing / socks

The _____ was much taller than the goat.

frog / mouse / giraffe

Charlotte gave her dog a _____.

fish / treat / spade

Steve had a _____ about a unicorn.

chord / costume / dream

mystery words

Take the initial sound or digraph from each picture to work out the mystery words.

For example:

ea from eat	**g** from gate	**l** from lamp	**e** from egg

eagle

ch from chair	i from igloo	p from pear	s from sock

chips

clue: you might have them with fish

sh	a(corn)	d(rum)	e

shade
shade

clue: when it is sunny you might like this

p	r	ow(l)	l

prawl

clue: a panther might do this

sounds like ... ai in train

The **ai** sound can be spelt in many different ways.

Circle the words that do **not** have the **ai** sound.

All the words below have the **ai** sound. Colour the squares for each pair of spellings in the same colour.

train	table	great	snake
game	reindeer	obey	eight
acorn	crayons	snail	grey
break	neighbour	veil	tray

sounds like . . . ee in bee

read

even

queen

happy

pizza

thief

key

Circle the words that do **not** have the **ee** sound.

shield

fly

theme

bread

bee

steam

honey

ivy

turkey

donkey

leaf

sea

A Sailor Went to Sea

A sailor went to sea, sea, sea,
To see what he could see, see, see.
But all that he could see, see, see,
Was the bottom of the deep blue sea, sea, sea!

sounds like . . . igh in fright

fright

fried

surprise

spy

These words have the same vowel sound but are spelt differently. Write each word.

igh

ie

i–e

y

sounds like . . . oa in boat

The **oa** sound can be spelt in many different ways.

Circle the words that do *not* have the **oa** sound.

home

doe

post

float

snowball

throw

shoes

bow and arrow

radio

pond

toes

telephone

blow

sounds like . . . oo in boots

The long **oo** sound can be spelt in many different ways.

Circle the words that do **not** have the long **oo** sound.

screw

flute

blue

chewing gum

blew

hoop

broom

flew

foot

kangaroo

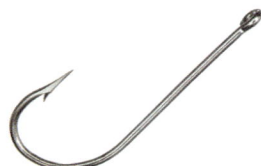
hook

flu

canoe

ruler

sounds like . . . oo in books

books **should** **cushion**

See how many words with the **oo** sound you can find in the word-search below. Circle each word when you find it.

p	y	s	h	o	o	k	p	w	q	c	b
u	w	o	u	l	d	h	h	o	o	k	r
t	k	b	u	l	l	r	h	s	m	p	o
v	u	n	d	e	r	s	t	o	o	d	o
f	o	o	t	s	a	f	u	l	l	p	k
p	u	l	l	h	r	i	y	j	c	u	k
w	m	b	s	o	w	o	o	l	o	s	t
o	a	u	x	u	l	q	n	c	o	h	w
o	j	s	i	l	h	o	o	d	k	g	i
d	m	h	j	d	g	n	c	o	u	l	d
s	c	r	a	p	b	o	o	k	q	g	x
l	v	a	p	c	u	s	h	i	o	n	t

sounds like . . . air in chair

bear

where

square

chair

Circle the words that do **not** have the **air** sound.

share

hare

tear

swimwear

wheat

hear

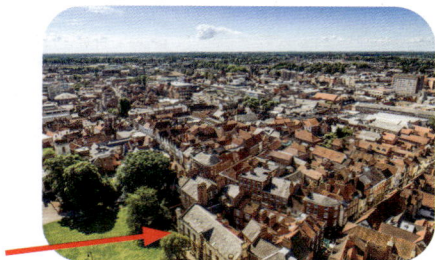
there

fair hair

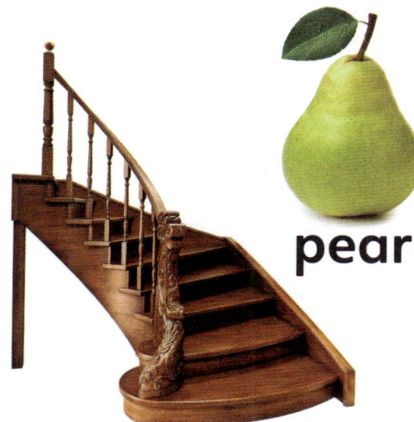
stairs

pear

sounds like . . . ear in clear

clear

deer

here

fierce

Join the words to the correct spelling.

pier

sphere

hear

skier

jeer

ere

ear

ier

eer

sincere

beer

year

spear

sounds like . . . ur in fur

All these words have the **ur** sound. Draw lines between the words that have the same spelling.

burn

fern

turn

learn

thirsty

water

earth

worm

bird

world

stern

worker

sounds like . . . oi in soil

All these words have the **oi** sound. Circle the correct spelling for each word.

foil   foyl

joi   joy

coyns   coins

boy   boi

toi   toy

point   poynt

oyster   oister

sounds like . . . or in fork

All these words have the **or** sound. Draw lines between the words that have the same spelling.

paw

door

walk

pour

talk

daughter

four

bored

horse

floor

saw

ball

corn

call

naughty

adore

sounds like . . . ow in cow

cow

round

plough

Circle the words that do **not** have the **ow** sound.

ground

flower

glow

owl

crow

down

sprouts

towels

count

bough

trousers

sounds like . . . ew in dew

dew

tune

argue

Circle the words that do **not** have the **ew** sound.

nephew

queue

computer

9
nine

new

statue

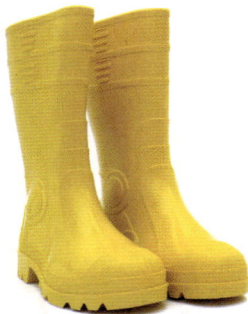
boots

tissues

tube

colour and match

a e j o u

Draw a line to join up all the word pairs with the same vowel sound (not the same spelling!)
Then colour in the pictures.

home

leaf

chair

horse

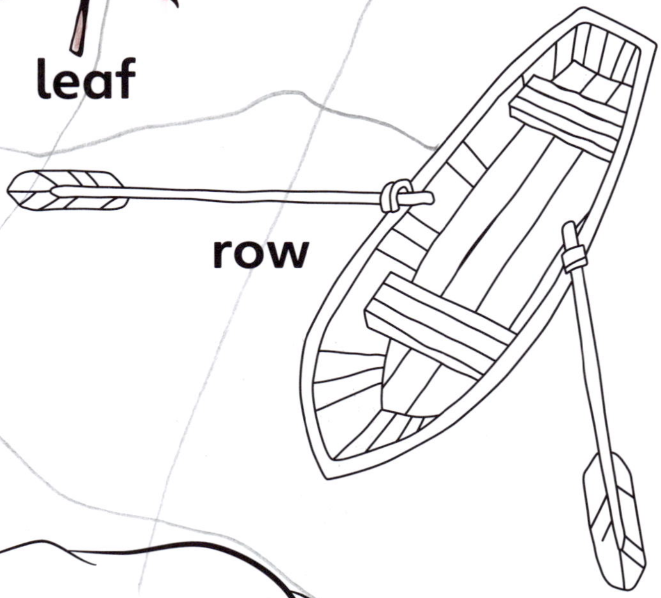

row

tree

bear

ball

bird

cake

shoe

rain

bike

flowers

fly

mouse

zoo

Earth

match the sound

Draw a line to join up the word pairs in each box with the same vowel sound.

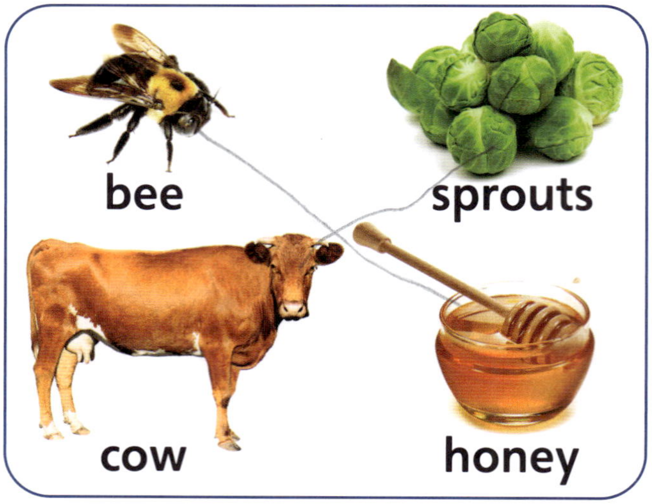

clear   pie

fright   deer

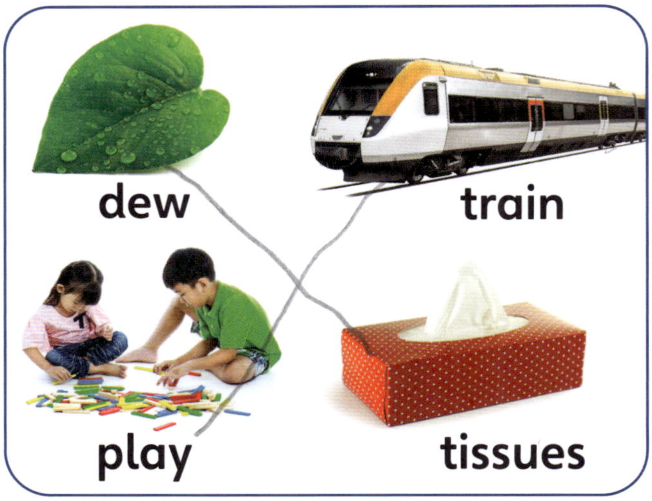

dew   train

play   tissues

canoe   snowman

boat   boots

cushion   horse

books   ball

water   burn

chair   bear

bee   sprouts

cow   honey

new phoneme . . . zh in treasure

treasure

television

These words have the **zh** sound. Draw lines between the pairs of words with the same spelling.

measure

casual

Asia

decision

Now practice writing the words.

treasure   television

casual   Asia

measure   decision

same sound, different spelling

sandwic**h**

witch**

All these words contain the same sound. Circle the pictures with the **ch** spelling in red, and those with the **tch** spelling in blue.

catch

stretch

teacher

beach

spinach

fetch

hutch

match

detached

same sound, different spelling

jug orange hedge gymnastics

Join the words to the correct spelling.

jump

bridge

plunge

fridge

hedgehog

giraffe

injured

allergic

village

ge

j

g

dge

gentle

same sound, different spelling

team

lamb

Join the words to the correct spelling.

combs

jam

m

climb

mb

crumbs

blossom

thumb

limb

mushrooms

ham

gum

same sound, different spelling

newspaper

knock

gnaw

Fill in the missing words.

The _____ wore shiny armour.

The _____ looks very sharp.

Sam hurt his _____ when he fell.

Grandad has a _____ in his garden.

Eve tied a _____ in her shoelaces.

A road _____ showed the way.

same sound, different spelling

rabbit

unwrap

Complete the words.

   wr + ap   = _____

   wr + en   = _____

wr + ite   = _____

wr + ong   = _____

   wr + eck   = _____

   wr + eath = _____

same sound, different spelling

The **s** sound can be spelt in different ways.
Join these words to the correct spelling.

nurse

celebrate

scissors

juicy

ice

crescent

soap

s

sc

ce

cy

ci

city

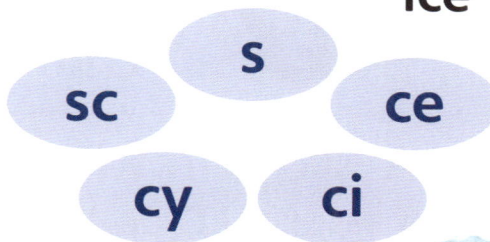
scent

icicles

cycle

pencils

mice

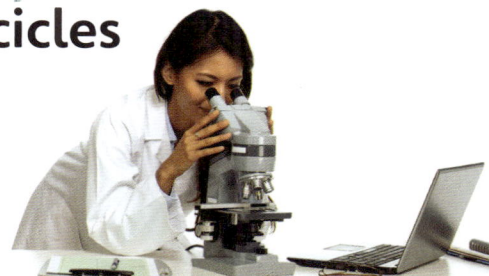
scientist

same sound, different spelling

The **sh** sound can be spelt in many different ways.

Join the pairs of words which have the **sh** sound spelt in the same way.

splash

sure

machine

chef

sugar

shell

Here are some more ways in which the **sh** sound can be spelt. Trace each spelling.

direction

musician

musician

delicious

direction

expression

delicious

expression

same sound, different spelling

The letter **v** can start a word. When it is written in the middle or at the end of a word it is usually followed by the letter **e**.

Join the words to the correct spelling.

van

vase

wave

leaves

beginning v

violin

middle/end ve

volcano

five

love

hive

gloves

Did you know?
Geese fly in the shape of a V. When the goose in front gets tired, another takes the lead.

when s says z . . .

Circle the words that do **not** have the **z** sound.

house

roses

cheese

hose

choose

noise

wasp

when ch says k . . .

Circle the words that do **not** have the **k** sound.

chip

anchor

school

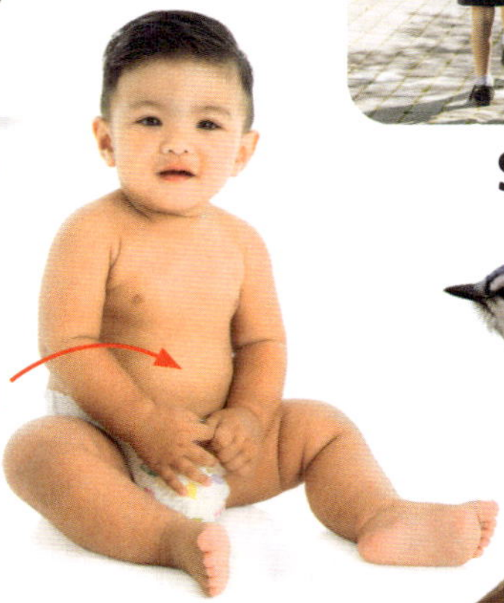

stomach

chemistry

perch

children

sounds the same, but . . .

These pairs of words sound the same but have different spellings and mean different things.

> see   night   pair
>
> pear   wail   sea   hair
>
> whale   hare   knight

Complete the sentences with the correct words.

Eve combs her _____ every night.

My grandad needs glasses to _____.

The blue _____ is enormous.

Alex fell over and began to _____.

The brown _____ jumped over the bush.

The brave _____ rescued the princess.

I love to holiday beside the _____.

Dad bought a new _____ of shoes.

We close the curtains at _____.

I prefer a _____ to an apple.

a phonic mosaic

Colour in the picture according to the code.

Words with wr, gn and kn* ▢ (orange)   Split digraph words ▢ (red)

Words with ph and wh* ▢ (green)   Words with zh phoneme ▢ (purple)

Short vowel sounds ▢ (light blue)   Nonsense words ▢ (black)

Words with wr, gn, kn, ph and wh should be coloured orange or green (as shown) even if they have a short vowel sound or a split digraph.

jump	drink	tent	parnt	dress	frog	crab	smole	bell	link	ring
sink	wrote	design	melt	brant	little	choop	crept	wrinkle	gnarl	spill
knee	gnome	photo	knife	said	loof	asked	knight	wheel	gnat	kneel
knit	when	knuckle	knock	reign	moob	sign	gnaw	wrist	dolphin	wring
lamp	knob	knead	signed	know	ranp	wrap	knot	wreath	write	shelf
bulb	swing	chat	unwrap	wreck	boam	wren	wrong	milk	belt	swim
chin	even	tune	cane	these	menk	rose	chase	slope	rule	flat
frame	spade	theme	kite	home	choaw	hide	skate	smile	slide	chime
cube	grape	treasure	flame	bike	frime	swede	stripe	decision	globe	cute
pillow	broke	nose	role	tape	santy	lane	hope	came	stile	chimp
fish	wig	plane	lute	blink	plime	shed	stale	ride	slap	plot

What is the picture of?

Writing

the alphabet

Trace all the upper case and lower case letters.

A A A A a a a a

B B B b b b

C C C c c c

D D D d d d

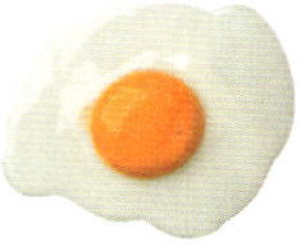

E E E e e e

F F F f f f

G G G g g g

H H H h h h

I I I i i i

J J J j j j

K K K k k k

L L L l l l

M M M m m m

N N N n n n

O O O o o o

P P P p p p

Q Q Q q q q

R R R r r r

S S S s s s

T T T t t t

U U U u u u

V V V v v v

W W W w w w

X X X x x x

Y Y Y y y y

Z Z Z z z z

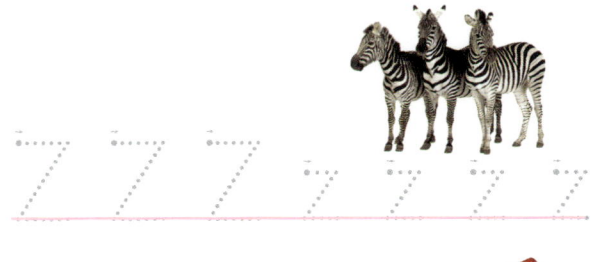

Now write your full name.

nouns

! A **noun** is a naming word. It names a person, animal, place, thing, or idea.

nouns		not nouns	
woman	school	funny	run
dog	book	soft	cloudy
happiness		are	see

Look at the things in the picture below.

Now circle each **noun.**

kite	sea	hot
swim starfish	bucket	sand
play	wet	sand

Complete the sentences with the missing nouns.

lorry	village	dog	apple

The _____ wagged its tail.

The _____ is yellow.

My friend lives in a _____ .

The _____ is red and shiny.

Write the nouns to finish the story.
For each sentence, choose the correct category.

football	brother
outside	ball

I like to play with my _____ , Jack. (person)

We play _____ . (place)

I can kick the _____ very hard! (thing)

It is fun to play _____ . (sport)

scrambled nouns

Unscramble the letters. Write the noun under each picture.

obta

inol

pipoh

rtian

sidel

palep

ohsre

ircah

dbrae

compound words

! A **compound word** is made up of two or more words.

butter + fly = butterfly

Join the words below to make a compound noun.

+ = _____

+  = _____

+ = _____

+  = _____

+  = _____

 +  = _____

syllables

! Words have parts, called **syllables**. Each syllable is like a beat. You can clap to count the syllables.

one syllable: sun   car

more than one syllable: happy   te le phone

Say each word. Clap and count the syllables. In each line, cross out the word with more than one syllable.

bird	cat	animal	fox
boat	dive	pool	water
five	eleven	one	nine

Say each word. Clap and count the syllables. Colour the right number of stars to show the syllables.

apple

butterfly

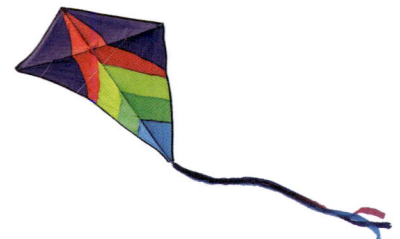

kite

adjectives

WRITING

! **Adjectives** describe nouns. They tell us what someone or something is like.

shiny   purple   tasty   gold   curved
playful   warm   cold   colourful   soft

Use two of the words above to describe each picture.

The toy crown is _____ and _____.

Those _____ gloves look _____.

My _____ umbrella has a _____ handle.

My kitten is _____ and _____.

Icecream is _____ and _____.

Did you know?
The first umbrellas were made thousands of years ago, in China, Egypt, and Greece. But ancient umbrellas were used to keep off sun, not rain!

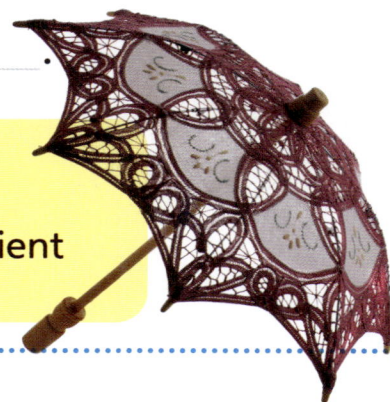

plurals

! **Plural** means more than one. You can add an **s** to most nouns to make them plural.

penguin

penguins

Trace each word, then make it plural.

elephant _____

pigeon _____

kitten _____

hen _____

rabbit _____

lion _____

Did you know?
A lion's roar can be heard more than five miles away!

! If a noun ends in an **'sh'**, **'ch'**, **'ss'**, **'s'**, **'x'** or **'z'**, add **'es'** to the end of the word.

bus → **buses**

Add the correct ending to make each word plural.

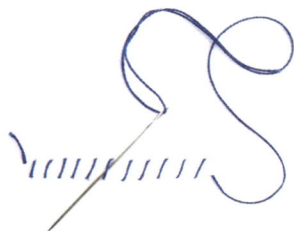

glass

stitch

dish

walrus

bunch

dress

peach

box

watch

An **'s'** or **'es'** at the end of a word can also show the *third person singular of a verb*, such as **'he eats'**, **'she walks'**, **'he catches'**.

Make these words plural.

	toothbrush		
	clock		
	cross		
	hat		
	guitar		
	fox		
	cake		
	sandwich		
	fortress		
	kitten		
	hutch		

the prefix 'un'

Write '**un**' in front of these words to make them mean the **opposite**.

lucky _____

happy _____

pack _____

wrap _____

Choose the right word to fit the meaning.

untidy	untrue	invisible	undress

cannot be seen _____

false _____

take your clothes off _____

messy _____

adding 'ing' and 'ed'

! Doing or being words are called **verbs**. We can change the tense of a verb by adding 'ing' or 'ed' on the end.

Add '**ing**' to each of these verbs.

walk

play

wait

Add '**ed**' to each of these verbs.

pull

help

wash

Choose the right ending to fit each sentence.

Yesterday the girls play____ football.

Toby is eat____ his dinner.

I pack____ my backback for school.

Evie is plant____ a flower.

adding the suffix 'er' to verbs

Make a noun by adding the prefix **'er'** to these verbs.

think   ⟶ _____

play   ⟶ _____

help   ⟶ _____

teach   ⟶ _____

climb   ⟶ _____

clean   ⟶ _____

read   ⟶ _____

using 'er' and 'est'

This giraffe is tall.

This giraffe is tall**er**.

This giraffe is the tall**est**.

Fill in the words below.

fast

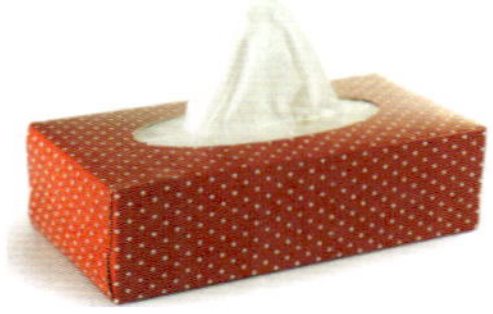

light

small

loud

contractions and apostrophes

> ! A **contraction** is when two words are put together, with one or more letters left out. An **apostrophe** shows where letters have been left out.
>
> he is ⟶ he's

Join each contraction to the complete words.

don't

can not

is not

I am

do not

can't

we're

isn't

I'm

we are

Finish the sentence with one of the contractions above.

The dog _____ fit through the door.

Add the apostrophe to each contraction

we will ⟶ w e l l

was not ⟶ w a s n t

I will ⟶ I l l

they are ⟶ t h e y r e

using 'and'

Complete the pairings below using 'and' and the missing word.

 +  fish _____

 + table _____

 + bucket _____

 + bread _____

Add 'and' to the sentences below and complete them using your own ending.

I took an umbrella _____

_____

I went to the park _____

_____

Remember to leave spaces between the words!

proper nouns

A **proper noun** is the **name** of a certain person, place, or animal. It begins with a **capital letter**.

common nouns		proper nouns	
queen	dog	Queen Elizabeth	Scamp
girl	boy	Lily	Jacob

Circle the **proper nouns** in orange.

city	Sydney	day	Saturday
bridge	Tower Bridge	planet	Jupiter
holiday	Boxing Day	month	July

The days of the week, months of the year, and the personal pronoun 'I' are all proper nouns.

Circle the correct form for each of these nouns.

Earth *or* earth

Frog *or* frog

japan *or* Japan

Did you know?
The word **Earth** is a *proper noun*. It is our planet's name! The word **earth**, without a capital letter, is a *common noun* that means land or soil.

days of the week

Trace the sentences, then copy them below.

On Monday, Maya made music.

On Tuesday, the twins tidied up.

On Wednesday, William got wet.

On Thursday, Thea was thirsty.

On Friday, Finn played football.

On Saturday, Sophia will be six!

On Sunday, Sam went swimming

Now write your own sentences, one for each day of the week. They don't have to be true!

Put a full stop at the end!

On Monday, I _____

On Tuesday, I _____

On Wednesday, I _____

On Thursday, I _____

On Friday, I _____

On Saturday, I _____

On Sunday, I _____

Did you know?
In English, the days of the week are named after gods in Norse mythology, except for Saturday, which is named after a Roman god. Monday is named after the Moon, while Sunday is named after the Sun.

How many days are there in the week? ☐

Which two days make up the weekend?

_____ and _____

punctuating sentences

Copy the sentences below adding in a **capital letter** at the start and a **full stop** at the end.

Always use a capital letter for 'I'.

i like to play tennis with sam

the beach was very busy on sunday

my sister and i both have dark hair

when it is cold i wear gloves and a hat

Split the long sentences below into two sentences and add punctuation.

the postman came to the door the dog barked angrily

the party on saturday was fun we played lots of games

! When we write a question, we need to put a **question mark** at the end of the sentence. We use **exclamation marks** for surprise or excitement.

Finish these sentences correctly with a **full stop**, **question mark**, or **exclamation mark**.

I like going to the circus ☐

Would you like to come, too ☐

When does it start ☐

The circus tent is very big ☐

The clowns are hilarious ☐

Would you like a snack ☐

How does the acrobat do that ☐

We saw a lion ☐

I enjoyed it very much ☐

scrambled sentences

The words in these sentences got mixed up! Write each sentence with the words and punctuation in the correct order.

Dad fixed toy the.

My blocks down fell.

guess who you is? it Can

cake Chocolate yummy is!

cold! The is of glass water

loves to Katie read.

tricky words

Complete the sentences by adding in the right word.

| called | people | oh | Mrs | their |
| asked | Mr | could | looked |

Daisy _____ a question.

_____ should recycle more.

Harry _____ Mia on the phone.

My teacher's name is _____ Jones.

Mr and _____ Hill like games.

Immy _____ jump really high.

They washed _____ hands well.

Josh _____ for a clue.

_____ dear! The egg is broken.

Watch out for capital letters!

silly sentences

Each sentence has one word wrong. Circle the wrong word, then write the sentence again so that it makes sense.

They gathered up the fish.

Felix flew the cart up the hill.

James made a huge biscuit.

Lucy picked ripe caterpillars.

They swam out of school.

Theo watered the cake.

Maddie splashed in the mud.

Riley hid behind the bed.

Elijah likes to wash his bike.

Ava loves her pet alligator.

Daniel's apple was smelly.

look, say, cover, write, check

For each of the common exception words below, read the word, say it out loud, then cover it with some paper or your hand. Next write the word down, and finally check to see if you got it right.

Look and **say**	Cover and **write**	Check and **write again**
the		
they		
love		
are		
were		
was		
here		
there		
where		

Look and **say**	Cover and **write**	Check and **write again**
put		
pull		
she		
said		
says		
friend		
your		
come		
school		
once		
today		
house		

my favourite animal

What is your favourite animal? Is it one of the animals above, or is it something else?

Where does it live? (in your house, in the wild ...)

How big is it? (as big as a ..., smaller than a ...)

What does it look like? Use three adjectives to describe it.

a day out

Think about a fun day out that you have had.

Where did you go?

Who did you go with?

What did you do there?

Use three adjectives to describe your day out.

Draw a picture of something you did.

what is happening?

Choose one of the titles below for each picture.
Then answer the questions.

> **A Visit to the Dentist**   **School's Out!**
> **First Day of School**   **Learning to Ski**

How do you think the children are feeling and why?

How do you think the boy is feeling?

Have you been to the dentist? How did you feel?

Why do you think the children are running?

Where do you think they might be going?

How do you think the children are feeling?

How did you feel when you tried out something new?

Did you know?
Top speed skiers can ski faster than a road car!

how to brush your teeth *(for aliens!)*

Imagine some aliens have come to visit. Explain to them how to brush your teeth.

Step 1

Step 2

Step 3

what happens next?

Cut out the sentences on page 353 to make a story about each picture. Finish the last sentence yourself.

a funny story

Fill in the blanks with words from the word box to make a funny story.

elephant dinosaur lion playground park
huge grey scaly green furry golden street
friendly hungry salad
lonely icecream
shy messy muffins

Did you see the _____ in the _____? I could hardly believe my eyes!

It was _____ and _____.

At first I was scared, but it was very _____, so I took it back home for tea.

It was very _____. It especially liked the _____!

Which animal did you choose? _____

Circle all the adjectives in your story.

Draw a picture of your new animal friend having tea with you.

What do you think happened afterwards? Write about what might have happened next.

scrambled story

Number the sentences [1–5] to tell this story in order.

☐ She asked Dog to help, but he said he was too tired.

☐ When Dog and Cat asked for some bread, it was Hen's turn to say 'no'!

☐ Once upon a time, a hen wanted to make bread.

☐ She asked Cat to help, but she said 'no', too.

☐ Poor Hen made the bread all by herself.

beginning, middle and end

The pages of this story are all mixed up! Read each page. Write **1** on the page that tells the **beginning**. Write **2** on the page that tells the **middle**. Write **3** on the page that tells the **end**.

Amy dropped her food. "Oh, no!" she said.

"It's okay," Zach said. "We can share my lunch."

Amy didn't know that her shoes were untied.

She tripped on her shoelaces.

Amy got her lunch.

She started walking to a table.

finish the story . . .

Here is the beginning of a famous story. Read the start, then answer the question.

the beginning

The Tortoise and the Hare

Once upon a time, there were two friends. Hare was very fast, but Tortoise was very slow.

One day, Hare was teasing Tortoise for being so slow. "It takes you forever to get anywhere!" Hare said.

"I get there in plenty of time," said Tortoise. "And I'll race you to prove it."

What are the names of the characters in the story?

_____ and _____

Read on.

the middle

Hare ran off quickly through the countryside and was soon far ahead of plodding Tortoise. Hare was so far ahead that he decided to stop for a nap!

Why did Hare take a nap?

Read on.

the end

Meanwhile, Tortoise kept walking slowly and steadily. Hours passed. He saw Hare, sound asleep by the side of the path . . .

What do you think happened next? Write the end of the story yourself.

write your own story

Using the pictures below to guide you, write your own short story about Nina's day at the beach.

What do you think happened to the first ice cream?

Write a short story about anything you like. It could be about dinosaurs, aliens, a new pet, a trip . . . anything at all!

First, draw your own storyboard pictures.
Have a **beginning**, a **middle** and an **end**.

Now write the story.

poets' corner

There are lots of different sort of poems. Here is an **acrostic** poem, where the first letters spell a word when you read down. That word tells what the poem is about.

Curious

Athletic

Tabby

What is this poem about? ....

Choose one of these words and write your own acrostic poem.

| DOG | HAPPY | RAIN | DAD | MUM |

Lots of poems rhyme (they have the same end sound)—but they rhyme in lots of different ways!

As I stood beside the sea,

I saw the dolphins leap in glee.

The water splashed and sparkled bright,

It was a truly lovely sight.

Which words rhyme with one another above?

_____ and _____

_____ and _____

Using one of the rhyming word banks below, write your own rhyming poem.

cat mat hat splat
rat pat that bat

frog log bog dog

grey day play way
stay say anyway

book review

Think about a book that you have read.
Write or circle your answers.

Title of the book: _____

Author of the book: _____

What kind of book was it?

storybook   picture book   information book

What was it about? _____

_____

_____

Rate the book by colouring 1 to 5 stars.
The more stars you colour, the more you liked it!

☆ ☆ ☆ ☆ ☆

Why did you rate the book the way you did?
Write two reasons.

_____

a thank you note

Imagine you have just had your birthday.
Your Granny and Grandad bought you a great
present. Write them a short letter to say thank you.

Start the letter, "Dear Granny and Grandad."

Thank them for the present.

Say what you want to do with it.

Say what you did on your birthday.

Finish the letter, "Love from ..." (write your name)

correcting your own work

Write three sentences about something you did last weekend. Write quickly—you will correct it later.

Look over your work carefully. Check your spelling.
Check for capital letters and punctuation.
Mark up any corrections.

Now write it out again below,
in your best handwriting.

Reading

the lion and the mouse

Read the story below, or ask someone to read it to you. Then answer the questions.

Lion was the fiercest animal in the land. One afternoon, when he was sleeping, a tiny mouse ran over his tail and woke him up.

Lion was angry. He wanted to eat the mouse. But Mouse squeaked quickly in fear, "Please, don't eat me! If you let me go, I promise I'll repay you one day!"

Lion thought this was so funny that he kindly let Mouse go. He chuckled, "How could someone so tiny ever help *me*?"

Time passed. One evening, Lion stepped into a hunters' net. He struggled and struggled, but could not break the net. He could not escape. He roared in anger.

One by one, the stars dimmed and faded as dawn approached. Lion felt hopeless. The hunters would soon come to get him. Then Lion heard a soft scurrying sound.

"Mouse?" he said, in surprise.

Mouse said, "Hold still." She patiently chewed through the ropes with her sharp little teeth.

"You saved me!" Lion exclaimed.

"One good turn deserves another," replied Mouse.

In the distance they could hear the hunters. "Let's get out of here!" said Lion.

Mouse nestled in Lion's thick mane. With powerful leaps, Lion carried them both to safety.

Who is the fiercest animal in the land?

Who is smaller, Lion or Mouse?

Why did Lion wake up?

Why was Mouse afraid?

How did Lion get caught?

How did Mouse rescue Lion?

Circle the key message of this story.

It is good to have friends with sharp teeth.

Lions are the best animals of all.

Everyone can be helpful, no matter their size.

Watch where you're going at night.

How do Lion and Mouse differ? How are they the same? Circle in red the words that describe Lion, and in blue those that describe Mouse. Which have you circled for **both** animals?

helpful   **big**   **small**

fierce   **kind**

Colour in the picture of Mouse rescuing Lion.

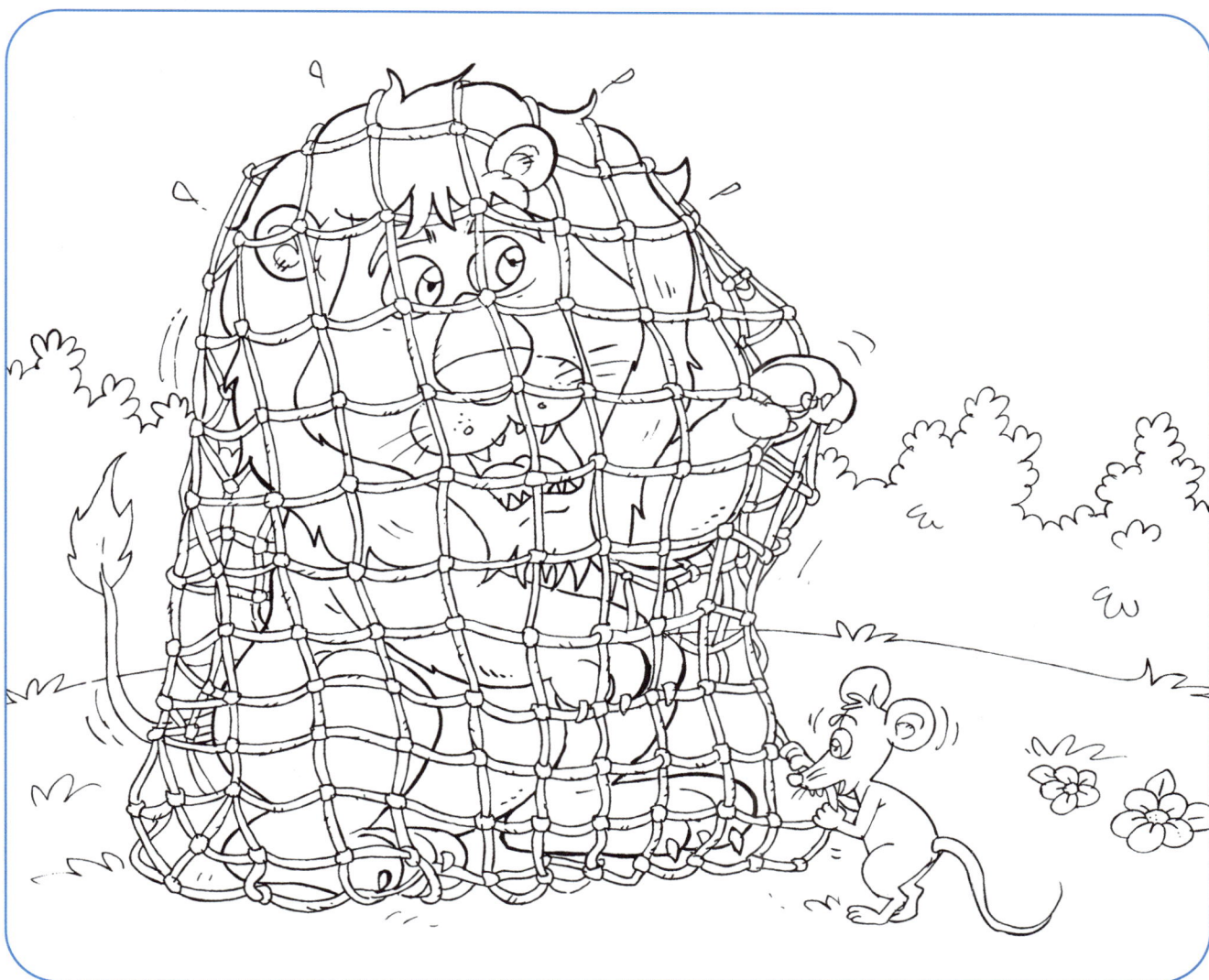

my cat

Read the poem. Then answer the questions.

My Cat

My cat likes her house.
My cat likes her mouse.
My cat likes to walk.
My cat like to stalk.
My cat likes to sleep.
My cat likes to leap.
My cat likes to see.
Most of all . . . she likes **me!**

Find a word in the poem that rhymes with each word below.

house *rhymes with* _____

stalk *rhymes with* _____

leap *rhymes with* _____

What, or whom, does the cat like best?

star light

Star light, star bright,
First star I see tonight,
I wish I may,
I wish I might,
Have the wish I wish tonight!

Write the answers to these questions.

What words in the poem rhyme with light?

What other words can you think of that rhyme with light?

What words are repeated in the poem?

Read the word at the end of each line. Which end word does **not** have a rhyming word in the poem?

Did you know?
The first star we see at night is often a planet, not a star! In fact, Venus is sometimes called the Evening Star. It looks much bigger than the stars because it is closer to Earth.

Sam and the seed

Read the text. Then answer the questions.

Sam got a seed.
He got a pot.
He put soil in the pot.
Sam dug a hole in the soil.
Sam put the seed in the hole.
He gave the seed water.
The sun shone on the seed.
A plant grew!

Circle the things that plants need to grow.

soil   log   hat   water
     milk   sun   bread

What happened **first**? Colour in the box.

☐ Sam got a pot.

☐ Sam dug a hole.

☐ Sam got a seed.

book club

New Book Club!

Do you like books?
We are starting a club.
We will share books that we like.
We will read new books.
Come to the school library on
Monday after school.
Bring a good book.

See you there!

Read the flyer, then answer the questions.

What is the club about?

Where will the club meet?

When will the club meet?

What book would *you* take to the club?

the amazing bumblebee

Read the text below, or ask someone to read it to you.

Bumblebees are bigger and fuzzier than other bees. Honey bees are smaller and less fuzzy. Bumblebees look furry and fat. They live in underground nests. They do not live in hives.

A queen bee starts the nest. She lays eggs. The eggs hatch and grow into worker bees. All worker bees are female. Their job is to gather food.

A worker visits a flower. She drinks nectar from the flower. She picks up pollen. When the bee goes to another flower, the pollen rubs off. The plants use the pollen to make seeds. Bees use pollen for food for baby bees.

Did you know?
A bumblebee flaps its wings 200 times per second!

Now answer these questions.

What do bees get from flowers?

Which is bigger, a honey bee or a bumblebee?

What does a baby bee eat?

Draw a bumblebee drinking nectar from a flower.

Turn to page 355 to make your own busy bumblebee!

hats, hats, hats!

Mrs Smith had a box.

The box was full of hats!

Min took a hat. It was pink and shiny.

Ben took a hat. It was blue and hard.

Dan took a hat. It was yellow with spots.

Sue took a hat. It was black with a red feather.

They had fun with hats!

Who took this hat?   Who took this hat?

Dan and Min traded hats. Circle the hat that Min has now.

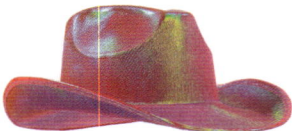

two girls, two stories

Read the texts below. Then answer the questions.

Lin's Story

Lin was happy. She took the football.

"Have fun!" Dad said.

Her friend Rob was outside.

"Let's play!" he said.

Lin and Rob had fun.

Jen's Story

Jen was excited. Today was a big day!

She put on her new kit and got in the car.

Mum drove to the football pitch.

"Good luck!" she said.

Jen ran to meet the rest of her team.

Circle the words that say how the girls are feeling.

How are the two stories alike?

_____

How are the two stories different?

_____

_____

man's best friend

Read the text below. Then answer the questions.

Dogs come in lots of sizes. There are tiny dogs that can fit in your pocket. There are big dogs that can't fit on your lap!

Some dogs can be trained to help people with disabilities. They help to keep them safe. These dogs are intelligent and loyal. Others can be trained to work with animals. Some dogs herd sheep.

Dogs are good friends. They like to play and cuddle, and are often very affectionate. They can also be very loyal. No wonder they are often referred to as "man's best friend"!

Circle each answer.

Does this text tell a story about a dog or give information about dogs?

information   story

Are all dogs the same size?

yes   no

What do dogs do for people? You can circle more than one answer!

keep them safe   cuddle   be friends

What job is this dog doing?

helping a person

protecting animals

Do you have a dog? If you do, draw a picture of your dog, or describe it in a few words. If not, then draw a picture or write about your ideal dog.

Did you know?
Dogs and cats can be very good friends with each other.

horsey, horsey, don't you stop!

Read the text below. Then answer the questions.

There are many kinds of horses. They do many jobs. They help farmers and police. People ride horses for fun and in sports such as polo and horse racing.

Before tractors were invented, the biggest and strongest horses worked hard on farms. They were used for ploughing and to carry goods.

Many horses are perfect for riding. Some horses are too small to ride, but people still love them as pets.

Baby horses, known as foals, can stand up within one or two hours of birth, and can gallop after about 24 hours! Race horses can run at more than 40 miles per hour!

What were horses used for on farms long ago?

Which can walk the soonest, a foal or a baby?

Look at the chart below. Then answer the questions.

Draft horses are big and strong.

Saddle horses are great for riding.

Miniature horses are under 1m tall.

Which horse would pull a farmer's plough?

Which horse is the shortest?

Which horse would a police officer ride?

seasons

Each year has four seasons.

Winter is the coldest season. Sometimes snow falls. We can skate on ice outside.

Spring is warmer than winter. Plants grow leaves and flowers. Birds sing and build nests.

Summer is hot. School ends for the year. It is great to cool off with a swim.

Autumn is cooler than summer. Leaves fall off trees. Birds fly away. We know that winter is coming again.

Which is the warmest season?

In which season do leaves fall off trees?

When do birds build nests?

What is *your* favourite season? Circle your answer.

spring   summer   autumn   winter

Draw a picture of something you do during your favourite season, and write about it.

noughts and crosses

! Some texts tell us how to do or make things.

Read the instructions below.

Noughts and Crosses

Do you have a pencil? Do you have paper? Then you've got everything you need to make a game!

Draw two lines down. Draw two lines across.

You be X. A friend can be O. Your friend will make an O. Then you make an X.

Take turns. Try to get three X marks in a row. Your friend will try to get three O marks in a row.

Whoever gets three in a row first wins!

Did you know?
Noughts and crosses is one of the oldest board games still played today. It started with the Romans, and the game was called *terni lapilli*, or three pebbles at a time.

Now answer these questions.

What do you need to play noughts and crosses?

_____

What shapes do you make in the game?

_____

How do you win noughts and crosses?

_____

Here is some space for you to play the game!

a mixed-up smoothie

Read the instructions for making a smoothie. The middle steps are out of order. Write 1, 2, 3, 4, or 5 in each empty box to put the steps into the correct order.

☐ *Cut up strawberries and a banana.*

☐ *Blend the fruit and yogurt.*

☐ *Pour into a glass.*

☐ *Add yogurt to the fruit.*

☐ *Put the banana and strawberries in a blender.*

6 *Enjoy!*

Write or circle your answers.

Which two ingredients are **fruits**?

_____ and _____

Which two of these foods are also fruits?

milk   peach   cracker   blueberry

Numbers

numbers 1 to 10

Count the animals. Then join them to the correct number. Finally, trace the word below the number.

1
one

2
two

3
three

4
four

5
five

6 six

7 seven

8 eight

9 nine

10 ten

numbers 11 to 20 . . . and 0

Count the objects. Then join them to the correct number. Finally, trace the word below the number.

11
eleven

12
twelve

13
thirteen

14
fourteen

15
fifteen

16
sixteen

17
seventeen

18
eighteen

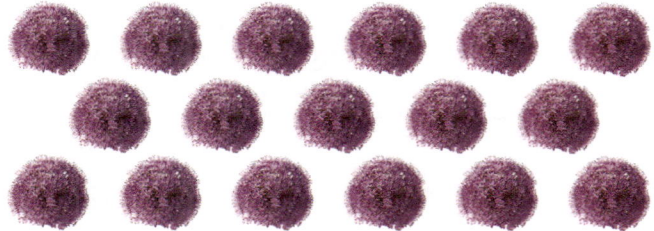

19
nineteen

20
twenty

← In this nest there are **3** eggs.

← In this nest there are **0** eggs.

0
zero

search and count

Count how many of each thing you can find below.

Write down how many of each item you counted.

a [ ]

b [ ]

c [ ]

d [ ]

e [ ]

f [ ]

all in order

Cut out the numbers on page 357, then stick them onto this page in the correct order, counting up.

dot to dot

Connect the dots in order to complete the picture.
Then colour it in.

42
41
43
44
40
45 46
47
2 3
39
48 49 50 1 4
5
38
6
37
7
36
8
35 27 26 25
9
28
24
34 29 23 13 12 11 10
30
33 32 31 22 21 14
20 15
19 18 17 16

Did you know?
Bees can sting a bear's face and ears.
They cannot sting through a bear's fur.

cold counting

Fill in the missing numbers in order. Then colour the boxes *you* wrote in (not the ones already filled in):

◼ for *your* numbers **less than 30**

◼ for *your* numbers **between 41 and 50**

◻ for *your* numbers **more than 83**

◼ for *your* numbers **between 61 and 70**

1	2	3					8	9	10
11	12	13					18	19	20
21									30
31	32	33	34	35	36	37	38	39	40
41	42	43		45	46		48	49	50
51	52	53	54	55	56	57	58	59	60
61	62	63	64	65					70
71	72	73	74	75	76	77	78	79	80
81	82	83		85	86		88	89	90
91	92	93	94			97	98	99	100

What have you drawn? ....

mind the gap

Fill in the missing squares on the number grid.

1		3		5	6	7		9	10
11		13	14	15		17	18	19	
21	22	23		25	26	27		29	30
31		33	34		36	37	38	39	40
41	42	43		45	46	47	48	49	
51	52	53	54			57		59	60
61		63	64	65		67	68	69	
71	72	73		75	76	77	78	79	80
81	82	83	84			87		89	
91		93	94	95		97	98	99	100

Count in 2s to fill in the missing squares on the number grid.

1		3		5		7		9	
11		13		15		17		19	
21		23		25		27		29	
31		33		35		37		39	
41		43		45		47		49	

Count in 5s to fill in the missing squares on the number grid.

1	2	3	4		6	7	8	9	
11	12	13	14		16	17	18	19	
21	22	23	24		26	27	28	29	
31	32	33	34		36	37	38	39	
41	42	43	44		46	47	48	49	

forwards and backwards

Use the ladder to help you count.

1 **Start at 15.**

a Count forward 3 = ☐
(up!)

b Count back 2 = ☐
(down!)

c Count forward 5 = ☐

d Count back 7 = ☐

2 **Start at 9.**

a Count forward 6 = ☐

b Count back 4 = ☐

c Count forward 3 = ☐

d Count back 5 = ☐

Now see if you can spot all the answers written as words in the grid. Circle each word when you find it.

t	n	m	t	w	e	l	v	e	s	p
w	i	y	p	s	q	m	l	u	o	y
e	i	g	h	t	e	e	n	y	y	f
n	b	t	h	i	r	t	e	e	n	i
t	r	c	f	o	u	r	p	i	q	v
y	y	p	r	v	b	m	n	g	i	e
w	f	i	f	t	e	e	n	h	u	y
s	v	r	e	b	n	m	o	t	w	a

Ladder numbers: 20, 19, 18, 17, 16, 15, 14, 13, 12, 11, 10, 9, 8, 7, 6, 5, 4, 3, 2, 1

number lines

Counting in 2s . . .

0 2 4 6 8 10 12 14 16 18 20 22 24 26 28 30 32 34 36 38 40

Fill in the missing numbers, counting forwards and backwards in steps of 2. Then colour in the pictures.

4   10   14   18

20 18   12   8 6

Counting in 5s . . .

0 5 10 15 20 25 30 35 40 45 50 55 60 65 70 75 80 85 90 95 100

Fill in the missing numbers, counting forwards and backwards in steps of 5. Then colour in the pictures.

5   15   30

60 55   45   35

Counting in 10s . . .

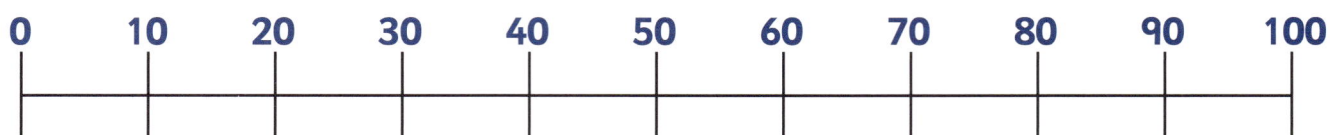

0   10   20   30   40   50   60   70   80   90   100

Fill in the missing numbers, counting forwards and backwards in steps of 10.

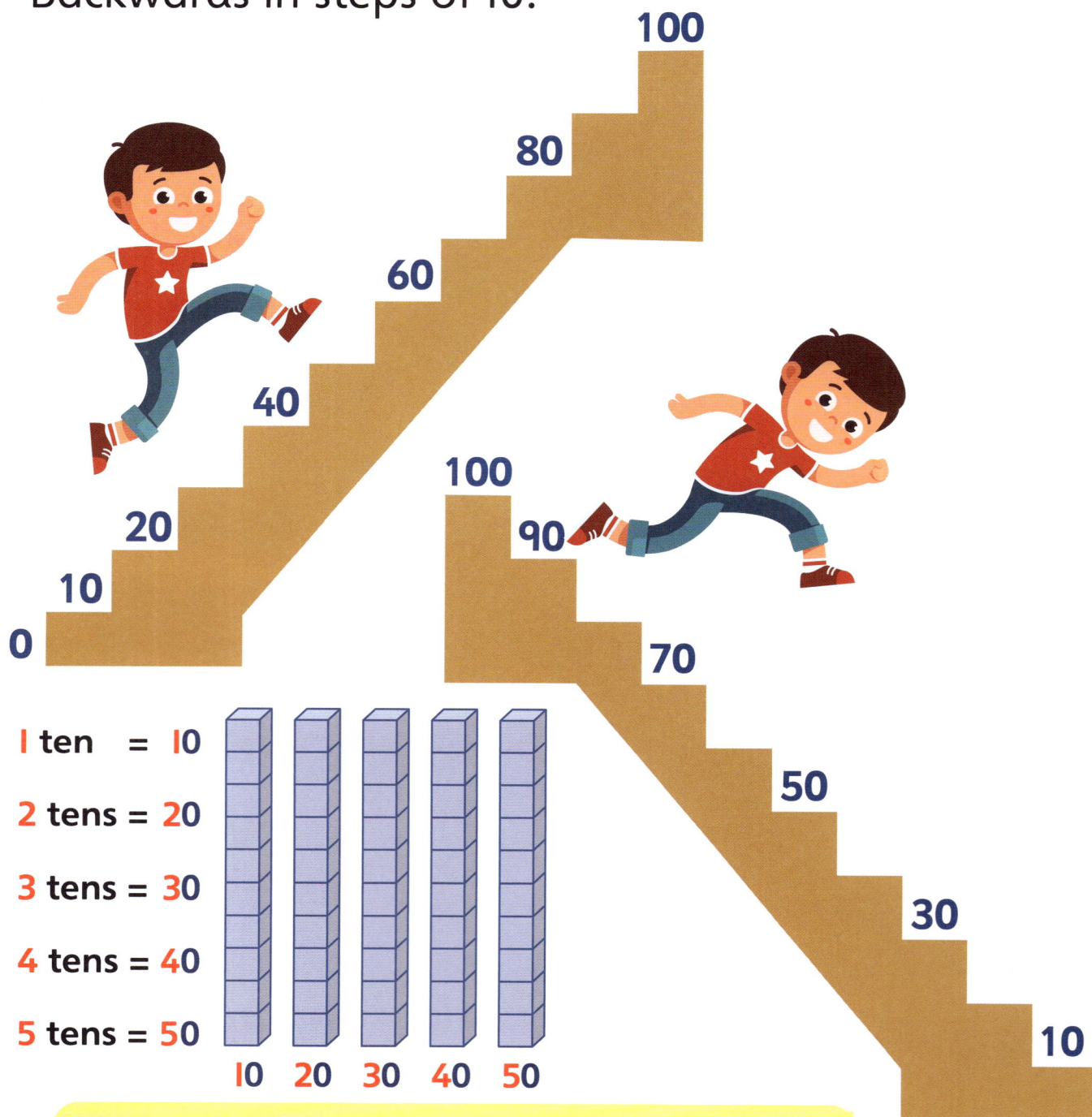

100
80
60
40
20
10
0

100
90
70
50
30
10

1 ten = 10
2 tens = 20
3 tens = 30
4 tens = 40
5 tens = 50

10 20 30 40 50

Did you know?
When you count by 10, every number ends in zero!

number maze

Count in 10s to help the clown make his way through the maze to find his balloons. Move one space each time, either diagonally or up or down.

22	43	55	70	100	
75	80	24	90	99	88
21	77	53	12	80	60
90	15	10	70	33	34
33	26	78	60	21	22
88	36	50	20	54	55
46	40	25	60	32	78
21	22	30	46	47	20
	19	20	8	9	10
	6	12	10	30	63
→	0	2	40	44

159

nutty counting

Help the animals to find their own path to the nuts by filling in the numbers.

20

50   100

80

14

35

12

60

25

8

20

30

10

4

10

2   0

0

0

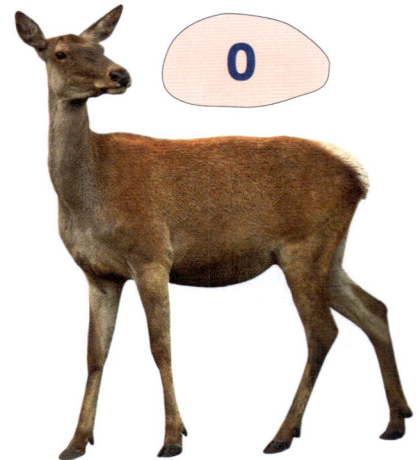

counting in 2s, 5s and 10s

1 Each koala has **2** fluffy ears!

How many ears are there in total?

How many ears would there be with **8** koalas?

2 Each stack of books has **5** books in it.

How many books are there in total?

How many books would there be in **10** stacks?

3 Each packet holds **10** crayons.

How many crayons are there in total?

How many crayons would there be in **3** packets?

4 Each box has **10** eggs.

How many eggs are there in total? ☐

How many eggs would there be in **7** boxes? ☐

5 Each bicycle has **2** wheels.

How many wheels are there in total? ☐

How many wheels would there be with **8** bikes? ☐

6 Each bunch has **5** balloons.

How many balloons are there in total? ☐

How many balloons would there be in **3** bunches? ☐

more or less

Join the numbers to the clues. Use the number line at the bottom of the page to help if needed.

16 25 19 11 27 18
30 21 13 24 14

a 29 is 4 more than this number.

b 13 is 3 less than this number.

?

c 15 is 3 less than this number.

d 15 is 2 more than this number.

?

e 12 is 1 more than this number.

f 25 is 2 less than this number.

?

?

g 28 is 2 less than this number.

?

i 25 is 1 more than this number.

h 20 is 1 more than this number.

j 23 is 2 more than this number.

?

k 11 is 3 less than this number.

10 11 12 13 14 15 16 17 18 19 20 21 22 23 24 25 26 27 28 29 30

counting apples

Count the apples. Complete the graph below.

Colour one block red for each red apple.
Colour one block yellow for each yellow apple.

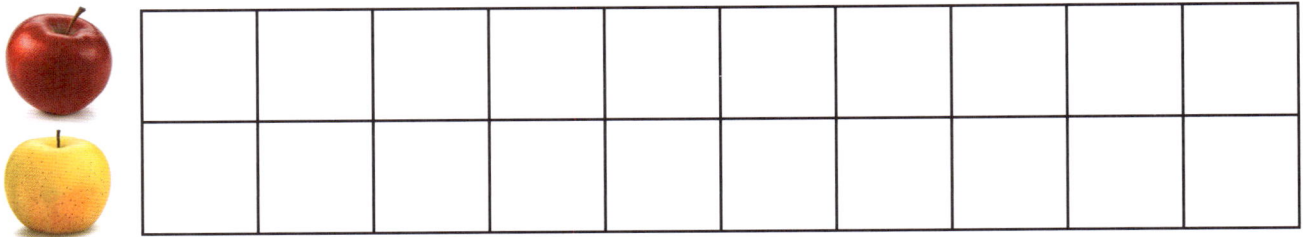

The graph shows how many children ate each colour of apple. Use the graph to answer the questions.

How many children ate apples?

How many children ate red apples?

How many children ate yellow apples?

How many more children ate yellow apples than red apples?

Did you know?
It takes about 10 years for an apple seed to grow into a tree and produce fruit.

odd and even

1

How many shells are there? ☐

Is the number odd or even? _____

2

How many fish are there? ☐

Is the number odd or even? _____

Fill in the **even** numbers.

| 1 | | 3 | | 5 | | 7 | | 9 | | 11 | |

Fill in the **odd** numbers.

| | 2 | | 4 | | 6 | | 8 | | 10 | | 12 |

Colour in the fish which have **odd** numbers.

32 30 17 25

21

18 29 42 35

place value

How many tens and ones are there?

1

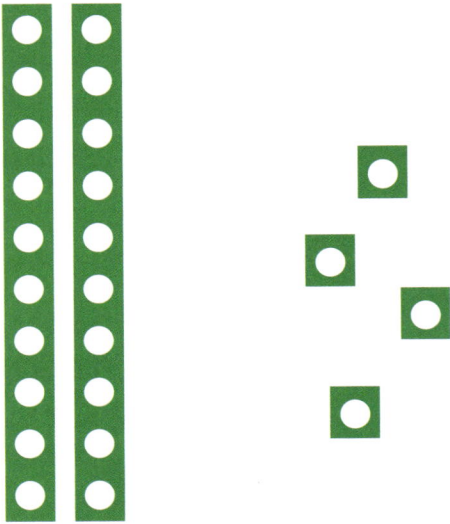

tens ☐   ones ☐

total (tens + ones) = ☐

2

tens ☐   ones ☐

total (tens + ones) = ☐

3

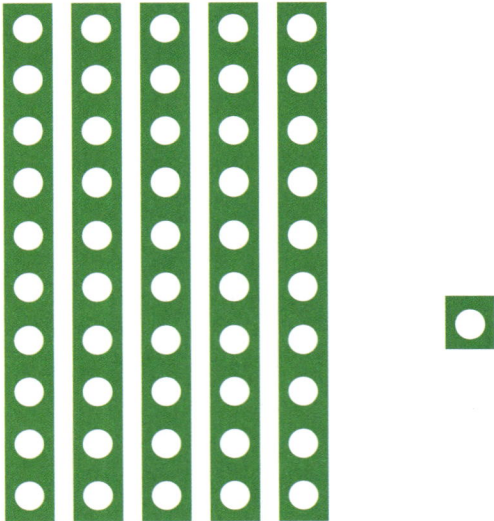

tens ☐   ones ☐

total (tens + ones) = ☐

4

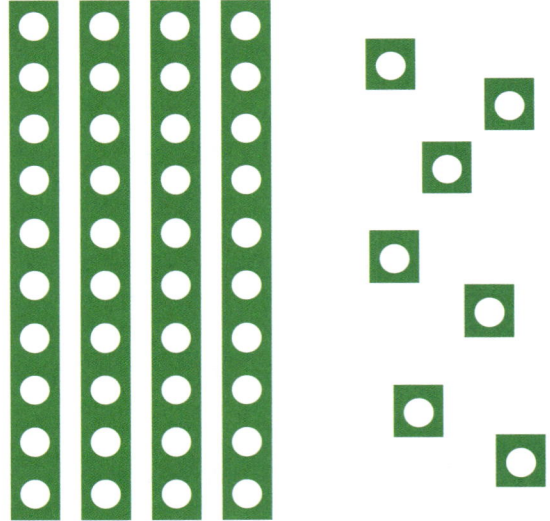

tens ☐   ones ☐

total (tens + ones) = ☐

crack the code

Count the bees, then write each number. Each number corresponds to a letter. Use the letters to answer the riddle.

	H

	S

	O

	U

	C

	B

	L

	Z

How do bees get to school?

by ___ ___ ___ ___ ___ ___   ___ ___ ___ ___
35 50 27 16 16 43   47 28 82 82

place value bingo!

Cut out the cards on page 359. Put them in a pile, face down. Choose one of the bingo cards below. Take turns with a friend to pick a card and match it to the number on your bingo card. There are 2 for every number! If it doesn't match, put it back. The first to cover all their numbers with both cards wins!

2 tens
5 ones

25

33	**50**	**41**
22	**26**	**37**

29	**43**	**30**
35	**18**	**21**

missing numbers—tens and ones

Complete the number triangles below by filling in the missing numbers.

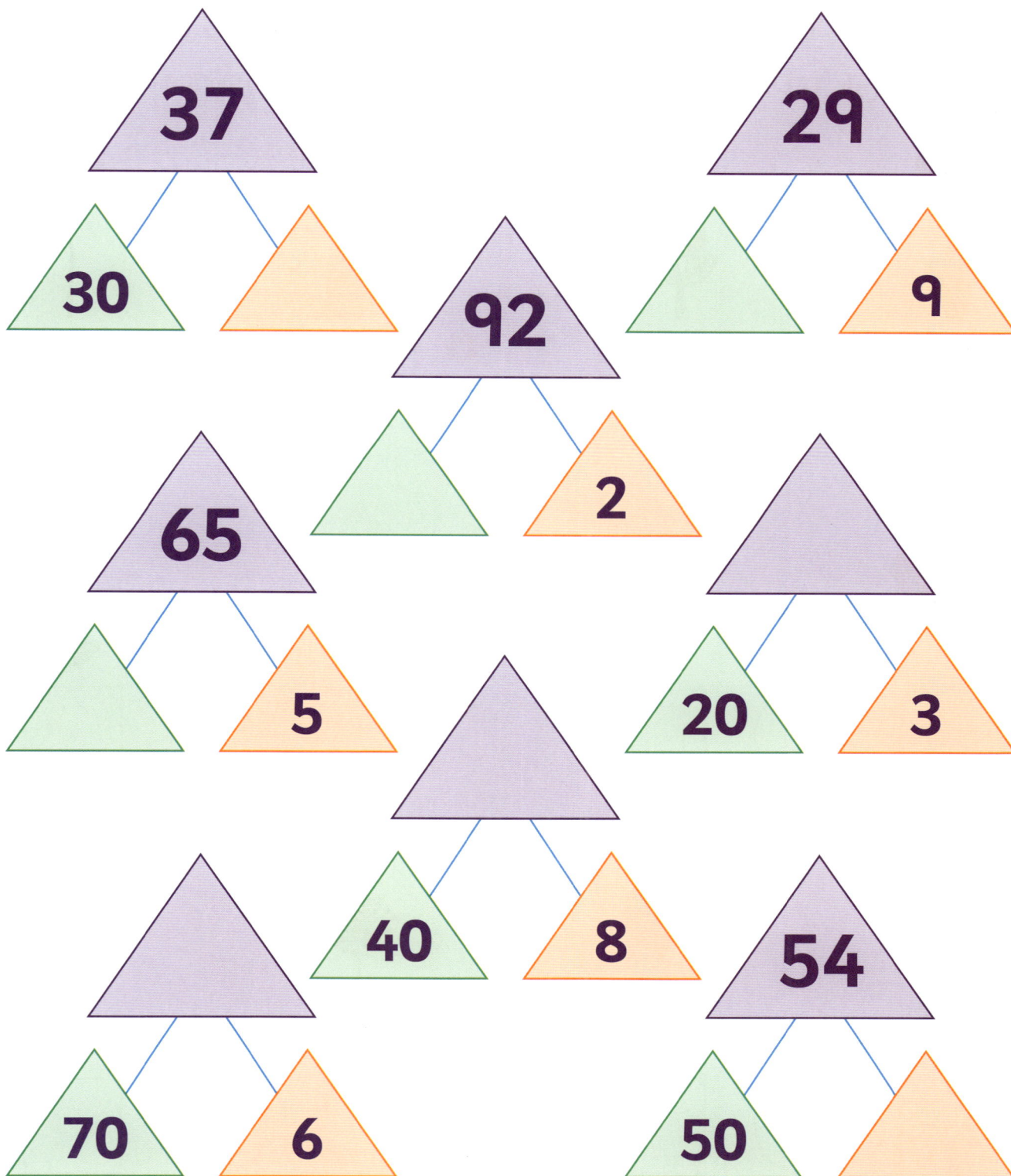

37 — 30, □

29 — □, 9

92 — □, 2

65 — □, 5

□ — 20, 3

□ — 40, 8

□ — 70, 6

54 — 50, □

flower power

Count the number of each kind of flower in the picture on the opposite page. Write the numbers in the boxes. Write <, >, or = in the circle. It might help to circle the groups of 10.

a.

b.

c.

d.

e.

f.

comparing numbers

Circle the two groups that are **equal** in number.

Circle the group that has the **fewest** in it.

Circle the group that has the **most**.

greater than or less than

To say that a number is **greater than** or **less than** another number in size, we can use symbols.

> 5 is greater than 3

< 3 is less than 4

Count the objects below, then draw the correct symbol in the middle to show which is greater.

Now use the correct symbol between these numbers.

| 47 | | 69 | 88 | | 59 | 33 | | 27 |
| 73 | | 91 | 64 | | 48 | 85 | | 91 |

ordinal numbers

In Chinese mythology, twelve animals competed in a race. The years in the Chinese calendar follow the order in which they finished.

Cut out the cards on page 361 and place them in the correct order. Trace the ordinal numbers.

Now answer these questions.

Which animal came **first**?

Which animal came **last**?

In what position did **Snake** finish?

In what position did **Monkey** finish?

Which animal finished in **seventh** place?

Which animal finished in **second** place?

Join the ordinal numbers to the correct words.

4th

7th

10th

2nd

1st

5th

6th

11th

8th

3rd

9th

12th

second
eighth
eleventh
first
tenth
fifth
twelfth
seventh
ninth
third
sixth
fourth

number puzzles

1 Jessica bakes 12 cupcakes for the school fair. Joel bakes 4 more than Jessica.

How many cupcakes does Joel bake?

How many cupcakes do they bake altogether?

2 A bee visits 14 tulips. There are 18 tulips in the garden.

How many more tulips does he have to visit?

There are 20 roses in the garden.

How many more roses are there than tulips?

3 A hen lays 5 eggs. The next day it lays 5 more, but the day after it lays just 1 egg.

How many eggs has it laid in total?

If Tom takes away 3 eggs, how many are left?

4 Pip gathers 8 apples from the tree.
His sister Polly gathers 6 apples.

How many apples do they have in total? ▢

Pip eats 2 apples. Polly eats 1 and gives 1 to a friend.

How many apples do they have left? ▢

5 James collects marbles. He has 12.
His father gives him 6 more.

How many marbles does he have? ▢

He loses 3 playing with a friend.

How many marbles does he have now? ▢

6 Sonia has 11 conkers. Jeb has 8.

How many more conkers does Sonia have? ▢

Sonia loses 2 conkers. Jeb finds 4 more.

How many conkers do they have in total now? ▢

7 Charlie and Chandra the chimpanzees have 7 bananas each.

How many bananas do they have in total?

Charlie eats 3 bananas, and Chandra eats 5. How many bananas do they have left?

8 Yasmin has 4 packets of crayons. Each packet has 5 crayons in it.

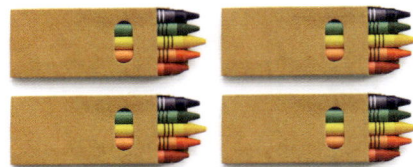

How many crayons does she have in total?

She gives 2 of the packets away to friends.

How many crayons does she have left?

9 Mo has 6 oranges, 6 limes and 6 lemons.

How many citrus fruits does he have in total?

He uses all the lemons to make lemonade.

How many fruits does he have left?

Arithmetic

addition

Write the answer, or draw the missing objects.

+  = ☐

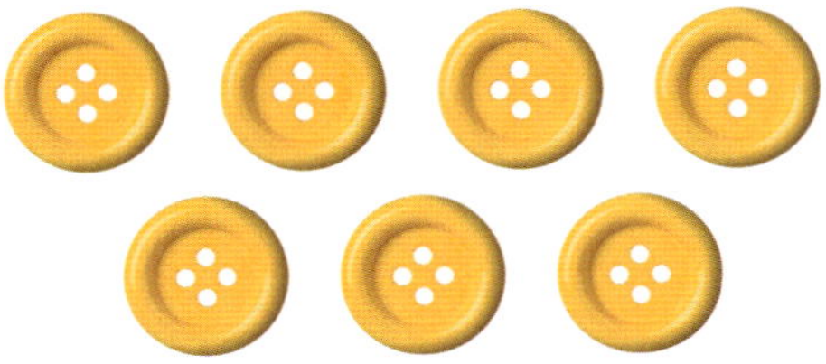

+ = 12

+  = 16

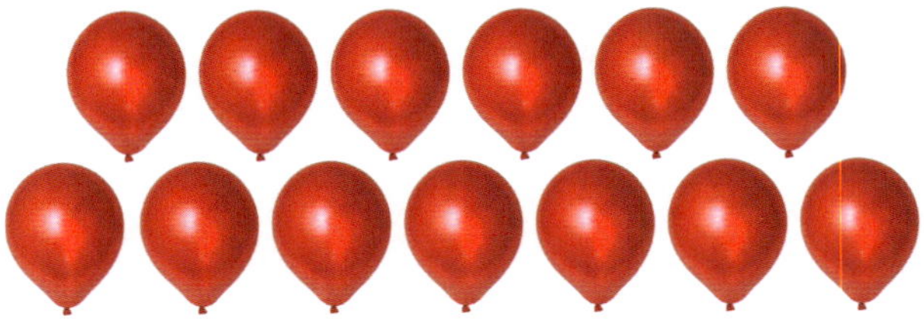

+ = 18

+  = 13

+  = ☐

kitten capers

Find out how many balls of wool each kitten has.
Write the numbers and add them together.

Ginger has [ ] + [ ] + [ ] = [ ] balls of wool

Luna has [ ] + [ ] + [ ] = [ ] balls of wool

Sooty has [ ] + [ ] + [ ] = [ ] balls of wool

Smokey has [ ] + [ ] + [ ] = [ ] balls of wool

Which kitten has the most wool?

more addition

Write the answer, or draw the missing shape.

a [8 dots] + [6 dots] = [ ]

b [2] + [3] + [ ] = 6

c [2] + [3] + [4] = [ ]

d [7] + [ ] = 16

e [10] + [8] + [ ] = 22

f [5] + [ ] = 15

g [9] + [6] + [3] = [ ]

h [ ] + [6] = 13

i [10] + [10] + [10] = [ ]

ARITHMETIC

maths on moths

Count the dots. Write the sum for each moth.

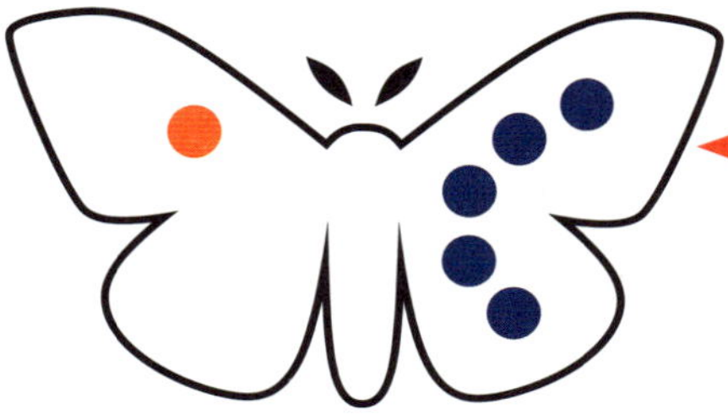

1 + 5 = ☐
5 + 1 = ☐

2 + 3 = ☐
3 + 2 = ☐

Now fill all the numbers in yourself.

☐ + ☐ = ☐
☐ + ☐ = ☐

☐ + ☐ = ☐
☐ + ☐ = ☐

What do you notice?

I can _____ in any order.

183

adding and comparing

Add the groups below. Then use the symbols >, < or = to compare the totals.

🐱🐱🐱 + 🐰🐰		🐶🐶🐶🐶 + 🐑🐑	
🥤🥤🥤 + 🍩🍩🍩🍩		🥛🥛🥛🥛 + 🍏🍏🍏	
👙👙 + 🕶🕶🕶🕶🕶🕶		🧢🧢🧢 + 🧣🧣🧣	

Add the numbers. Then use the correct symbol, >, < or =, in the middle to compare the totals.

3 + 3		5 + 2
4 + 3		3 + 5
6 + 2		4 + 4
5 + 4		7 + 0
8 + 2		2 + 7

number line addition

Use the number line to help you add numbers.

Example

9 + 8 = 17

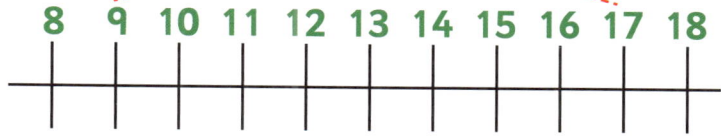

a 2 + 7 =

b 4 + 11 =

c 8 + 6 =

d 9 + 5 =

e 13 + 3 =

f 12 + 8 =

Now work out the missing numbers.

g 8 + [ ] = 16

h 13 + [ ] = 19

i [ ] + 13 = 18

j 11 + [ ] = 11

k 15 + [ ] = 19

l [ ] + 9 = 14

superhero scenarios

Read about the superheroes. Write the numbers in the boxes, then work out the answer to the question.

Juan's superhero can lift 6 adult elephants and 8 baby elephants.

How many elephants can his superhero lift?

☐ + ☐ = ☐

Layla's superhero can read 8 books and then 7 more books in the same day.

How many books can her superhero read in one day?

☐ + ☐ = ☐

Greg's superhero can run so fast that he passes 5 cheetahs and then 7 more cheetahs.

How many cheetahs can his superhero pass?

☐ + ☐ = ☐

Ava's superhero can learn to play 9 piano pieces and 9 flute pieces in one hour.

How many pieces of music can her superhero learn in one hour?

☐ + ☐ = ☐

Ellie's superhero can do 7 backflips and then 6 more backflips in a row.

How many backflips can her superhero do in a row?

☐ + ☐ = ☐

Arun's superhero can jump over 6 fire trucks and 9 more fire trucks lined up in a row.

How many fire trucks can his superhero jump over?

☐ + ☐ = ☐

Did you know?
People have been making up stories about heroes with special powers for thousands of years. Legends from ancient Greece and Rome tell of many powerful men and women.

crack the code

Write the answer to each sum. Each number corresponds to a letter. Use the letters to answer the riddle.

5 + 8 = ☐ **H**

10 + 5 = ☐ **R**

8 + 6 = ☐ **S**

9 + 9 = ☐ **T**

9 + 10 = ☐ **I**

8 + 8 = ☐ **E**

9 + 3 = ☐ **B**

10 + 7 = ☐ **D**

What did the squirrel eat?

___ ___ ___   ___ ___ ___ ___   ___ ___ ___ ___
18 13 16   12 19 15 17   14 16 16 17

hop on over

Add three numbers to reach 15.
Find different ways. Draw lines
to show how the frog can jump across the
pond. Use a different colour for each path.

2

15

7

5

3

6

3

5

6

5

6

3

9

subtraction

Write the answer, or draw the missing objects.

−  = ☐

− = 6

−  = 8

−  = 2

− = 5

−  = ☐

more subtraction

Write the answer, or draw the missing shape.

a ▮ − ▮ = ☐

b ▮ ▮ − ▮ = ☐

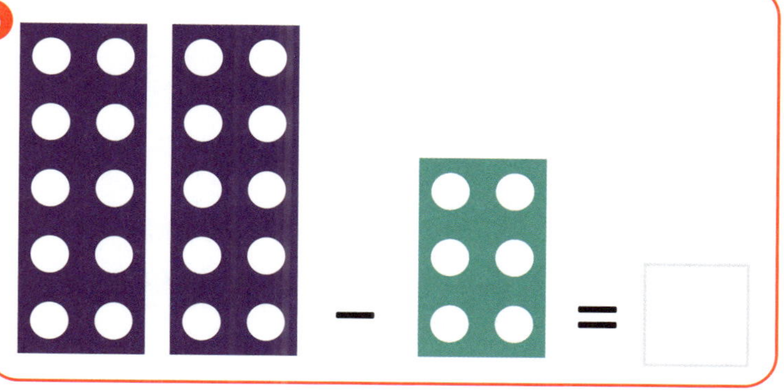

c ▮ − = 1

d ▮ ▮ − = 7

e − ▮ = 5

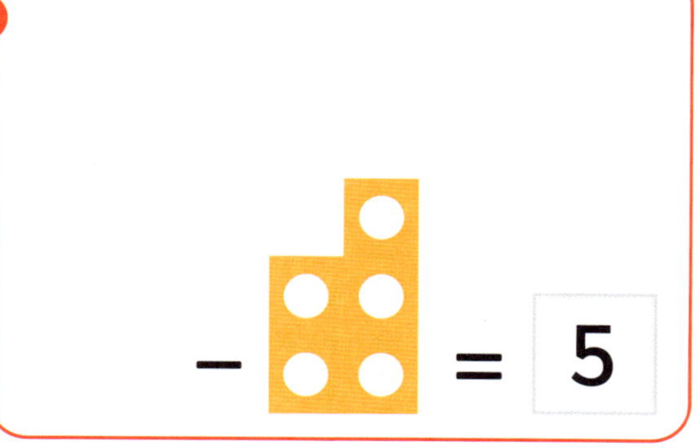

f ▮ ▮ − ▮ = ☐

g ▮ − = 4

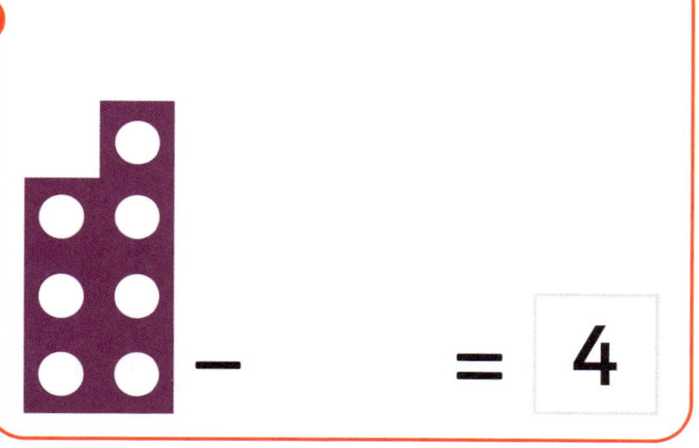

h ▮ ▮ − ▮ = ☐

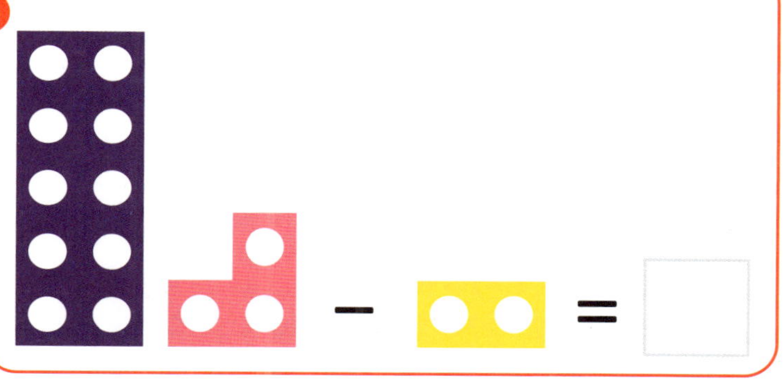

number line subtraction

Where does the ant stop? Count back using the number lines.

Example

$$12 - 3 = 9$$

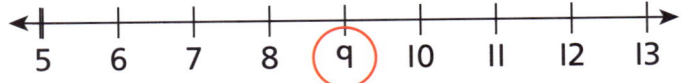

$$11 - 5 = \boxed{}$$

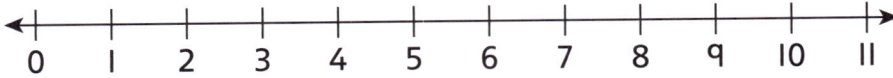

$$18 - 9 = \boxed{}$$

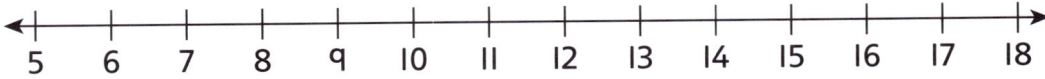

$$17 - 7 = \boxed{}$$

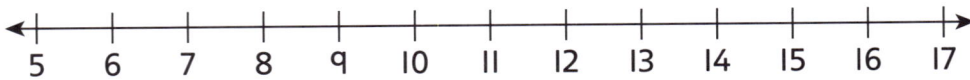

$$12 - 8 = \boxed{}$$

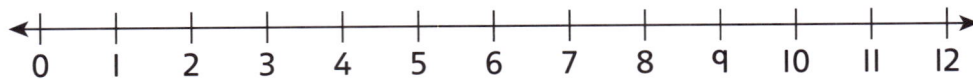

Did you know?
Ants have been around as long as dinosaurs!

crack the code

Write the answer to each sum by subtracting.
Each number corresponds to a letter. Use the letters
to answer the riddle.

8 – 3 = ☐ **I**

9 – 5 = ☐ **G**

5 – 4 = ☐ **S**

14 – 5 = ☐ **W**

15 – 13 = ☐ **L**

19 – 16 = ☐ **H**

9 – 3 = ☐ **C**

10 – 3 = ☐ **O**

5 – 5 = ☐ **A**

9 – 1 = ☐ **N**

What does Billy say on the phone?

___ ___ ___ ___ ___ ___ ___ ___ ___ ___ ___ ___ ?
9   3   7   5   1   6   0   2   2   5   8   4

mouse maths maze

Help the mouse find the cheese. Add or subtract.

Hint: The first answer is given.

Add 9 + 3 to find the next answer.

= 3 + 9

+ 6 + 3

+ 4

=

− = 1 = + 7

5 =

− =

5 + = 8 −

=

+

1 − 7 =

=

Write the number to finish the sentence.

The mouse [ ] the 🧀 !

using symbols

Does each question want you to add or subtract?
Circle the correct symbol, + or −. Then do the sum.

A plate has 6 pretzels.
Sam eats 3 of the pretzels.

How many pretzels
are left?

[ ] +
     − [ ] = [ ]

A bowl has 4 green grapes
and 4 red grapes.

How many grapes are in
the bowl?

[ ] +
     − [ ] = [ ]

A plate has 2 muffins. Oscar puts
5 more muffins on the plate.

How many muffins are
on the plate now?

[ ] +
     − [ ] = [ ]

A jar has 8 peanuts and
7 walnuts.

How many more peanuts
than walnuts are in the jar?

[ ] +
     − [ ] = [ ]

colour by numbers

Solve the calculations in the picture to work out which colour to use.

7+5

15–3

15–4   11–2   19–8

2+10

5+4   9+0

16–5   4+3   9–2   2+5   7+4

2+6   6+1

20–10   5+2   11–3   7–0

8–1   6+4

14–7

2+9   18–7   20–8

15–6   5+4   19–10

6+5

6+6

7	8	9	10	11	12
black	red	lime green	green	dark green	sky blue

hide the bunnies

! You can add and subtract using the same numbers.

Hide the green bunnies. Write the number of bunnies left.
Uncover the green bunnies. Write the number to add.

$$8 - 5 = \boxed{}$$
$$5 + \boxed{} = 8$$

Hide the blue bunnies. Write the number of bunnies left.
Uncover the blue bunnies. Write the number to add.

$$9 - 4 = \boxed{}$$
$$4 + \boxed{} = 9$$

Hide the red bunnies. Write the number of bunnies left.
Uncover the red bunnies. Write the number to add.

$$10 - 7 = \boxed{}$$
$$7 + \boxed{} = 10$$

Hide the yellow bunnies. Write the number of bunnies left.
Uncover the yellow bunnies. Write the number to add.

$$10 - 8 = \boxed{}$$
$$8 + \boxed{} = 10$$

Did you know?
Rabbits and hares have long ears to
help them keep cool on hot days.

number bonds

Complete the number bonds below by filling in the missing numbers.

20	20	20
12 / ___	___ / 9	10 / ___

20	20	20
___ / 1	___ / 13	5 / ___

20	20	20
14 / ___	___ / 0	___ / 3

20	20	20
___ / 11	18 / ___	___ / 4

number families

For each set of numbers, write 4 different addition and subtraction facts.

Example

9 balls

5 basket balls

4 beach balls

5	+	4	=	9
4	+	5	=	9
9	−	5	=	4
9	−	4	=	5

bugs

beetles

ladybirds

	+		=	
	+		=	
	−		=	
	−		=	

rubber ducks

yellow ducks

blue ducks

	+		=	
	+		=	
	−		=	
	−		=	

pens

red pens

green pens

	+		=	
	+		=	
	−		=	
	−		=	

number pairs

Complete the sums, then join the matching number families.

a 5 + 6 = ☐

b 8 = 15 − ☐

c 9 + 7 = ☐

d 8 + ☐ = 12

e 12 − 4 = ☐

f 8 = 11 − ☐

g 7 + ☐ = 15

h 16 − 7 = ☐

i 8 + 3 = ☐

j 11 − 6 = ☐

> Now play a game with number pairs!

Cut out the cards on page 363, and lay them face down. Take it in turns to turn over two cards. If the number values match, keep them. Otherwise turn them back over. The player who ends the game with the most pairs is the winner!

12 − 6

2 + 4

number puzzles

1 A shop has 15 mugs. All the mugs are blue or yellow. Five mugs are blue.

a How many mugs are yellow? [ ]

b 5 + [ ] = 15   **c** 15 − 5 = [ ]

2 The shop has 12 mugs with dogs on. Six have pug pictures. The rest have poodle pictures.

a How many mugs have poodles? [ ]

b 6 + [ ] = 12   **c** 12 − 6 = [ ]

3 The shop has 14 mugs with birds on. Five mugs have owls and the rest have parrots.

a How many mugs have parrots? [ ]

b 5 + [ ] = 14   **c** 14 − 5 = [ ]

4 The store has 13 mugs with dots or stripes. Nine mugs have dots. The rest have stripes.

a How many mugs have stripes? [ ]

b 9 + [ ] = 13   **c** 13 − 9 = [ ]

5 A clown has some balloons. Anna takes 5 balloons. He has 6 balloons left.

a How many balloons did the clown have before? ☐

b 5 + 6 = ☐   **c** ☐ − 5 = 6

6 The clown has some funny hats. He loses 4 hats. He has 8 hats left.

a How many hats did the clown have before? ☐

b 4 + 8 = ☐   **c** ☐ − 4 = 8

7 The clown has some bow ties. He gives 7 bow ties away. He has 8 bow ties left.

a How many bow ties did the clown have before? ☐

b 7 + 8 = ☐   **c** ☐ − 7 = 8

8 The clown has some party blowers. He gives 9 to another clown. He has 8 left.

a How many did the clown have before? ☐

b 9 + 8 = ☐   **c** ☐ − 9 = 8

ladybird halving

Use the ladybirds to work out halves.

half of **10** is

half of **8** is

half of **12** is

half of **18** is

half of **20** is

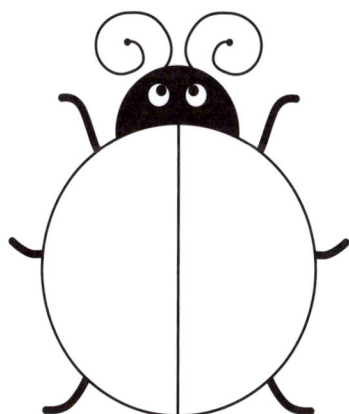

half of **16** is

multiplication by 2s

! In multiplication you take one number and add it together a number of times.

Each seal has **2** eyes. Count the eyes in sets of 2.

| 2 | + | 2 | + | 2 | + | 2 | + | 2 | = | 10 |

5 *sets of* **2**   or   5 x 2 = 10

Each dog has 2 ears.

How many ears are there?   7 x 2 =

Each bike has 2 wheels.

How many wheels are there?   4 x 2 =

Complete the table. The first row has been done.

2 + 2 + 2 = 6	3 sets of 2	3 x 2 = 6
2 + 2 + 2 + 2 + 2 = 10		
	2 sets of 2	
2 + 2 + 2 + 2 + 2 + 2 = 12		
	4 sets of 2	

Each array shows two multiplications. Write them.

⬜⬜⬜ (green, 6 dots)	3 x 2 = 6	2 x 3 = 6

(yellow, 10 dots)	☐ x ☐ = ☐	☐ x ☐ = ☐

(dark, 8 dots)	☐ x ☐ = ☐	☐ x ☐ = ☐

You can change the order in which you multiply the numbers, but the **product** (total) will stay the same.

(green, 6 dots)	☐ x ☐ = ☐	☐ x ☐ = ☐

multiplication by 5s and 10s

1 Each cake has 5 candles.

How many candles are there?

⬜ + ⬜ + ⬜ + ⬜ + ⬜ + ⬜ = ⬜

⬜ sets of ⬜ *or* ⬜ x ⬜ = ⬜

2 Each starfish has 5 arms.

How many arms are there?   ⬜ x 5 = ⬜

Each array shows two multiplications. Write them.

3    ⬜ x ⬜ = ⬜
⬜ x ⬜ = ⬜

4    ⬜ x ⬜ = ⬜
⬜ x ⬜ = ⬜

5    ⬜ x ⬜ = ⬜
⬜ x ⬜ = ⬜

6 Each girl has **10** fingers.

How many fingers are there? ☐ x **10** = ☐

7 Each bunch has **10** bananas.

How many bananas are there? ☐ x **10** = ☐

Each array shows two multiplications. Write them.

8

☐ x ☐ = ☐
☐ x ☐ = ☐

9

☐ x ☐ = ☐
☐ x ☐ = ☐

colour by multiplication

Solve the multiplications to work out which colours to use. Colour the edging in any colour you like!

10 x 10	11 x 10	3 x 10	5 x 5
6 x 2	2 x 2	2 x 5	9 x 2
11 x 5	3 x 5	2 x 10	4 x 2
7 x 5	8 x 10	8 x 5	5 x 10
6 x 5	2 x 12	9 x 10	6 x 10
3 x 2	8 x 2	4 x 5	2 x 3
4 x 10	7 x 5	7 x 10	12 x 5
10 x 2	2 x 4	5 x 2	7 x 2

0-10 light blue	11-20 turquoise	21-50 violet	51+ green

division

In division you split a number into equal parts or groups.

1 There are **8** biscuits to divide between **4** children. Divide them so each child has the same amount.

How many biscuits will each child get? ☐

2 How many toy cars would you need for **7** children to get **2** each? ☐

3 There are **9** apples to divide between **3** horses. Divide them so each horse has the same amount. Circle the apples in groups.

How many apples will each horse get? ☐

4 There are **10** crayons to share between **5** children. Divide them so each child has the same number.

How many crayons will each child get? ☐

5 How many eggs would you need for **6** chefs to use **2** each? ☐

6 How many sunflowers would you need for **4** bees to visit **2** each? ☐

7 There are **12** sweets to divide between **4** children. Divide them so each child has the same amount. Circle the sweets in groups.

How many sweets will each child get? ☐

fractions

! A fraction is a part of a whole number, and a way to split up a number or object into equal parts.

2 equal parts   half

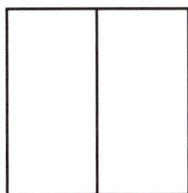

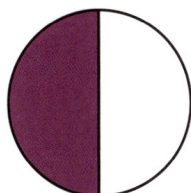

4 equal parts   quarter

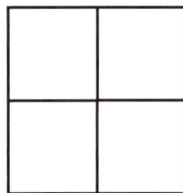

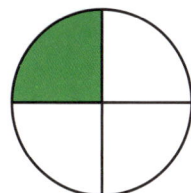

Draw a line on each shape to show **2 equal** parts.

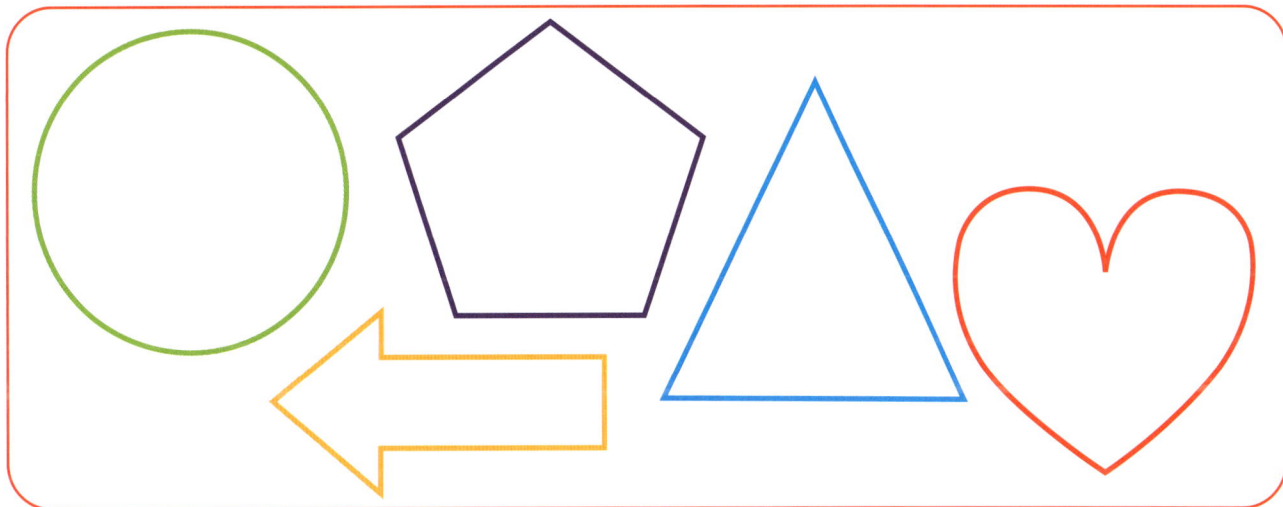

Draw lines on each shape to show **4 equal** parts.

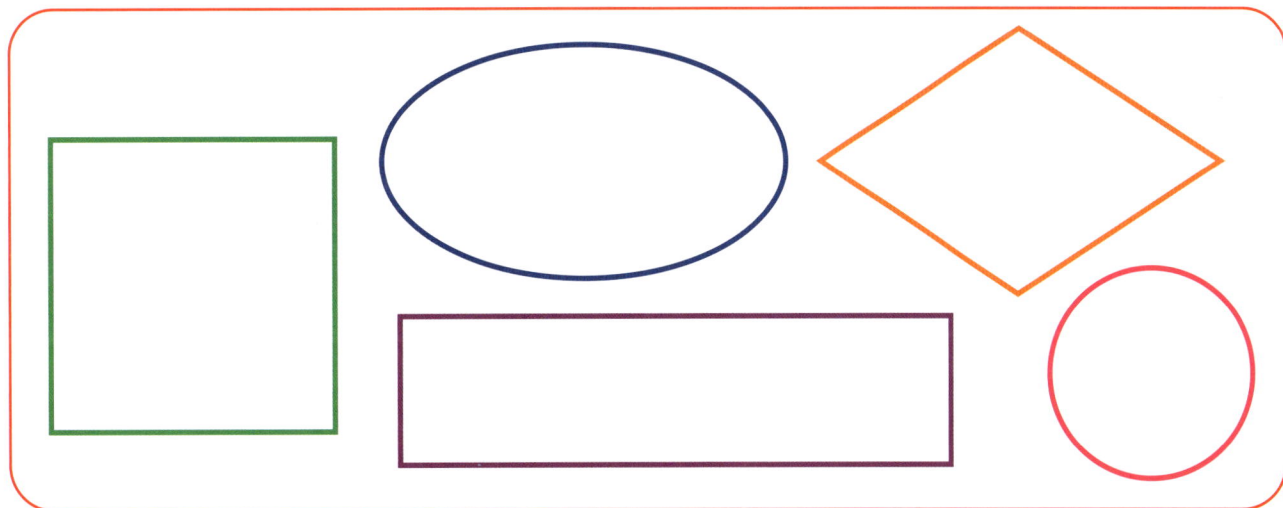

Is the snack being cut into equal shares?
Circle the correct answer.

a

yes   no   yes   no   yes   no

b

yes   no   yes   no   yes   no

Draw a line from each group to the pizza cut for them.

c

In which group will each child get a larger piece?
Circle that group.

Colour the fractions.

one quarter

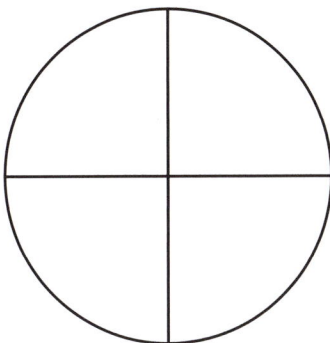

one half

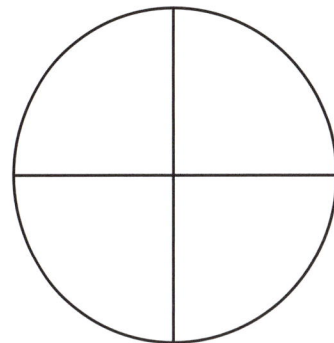

three quarters

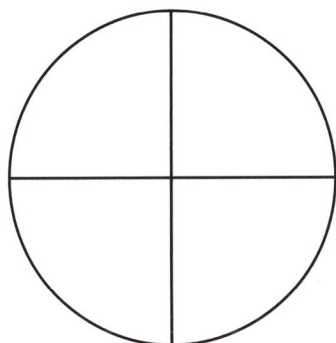

whole

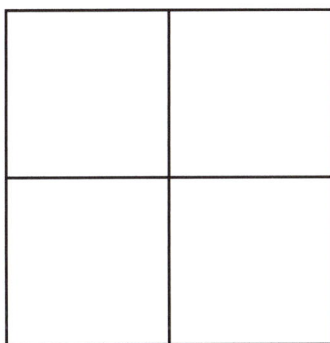

three quarters

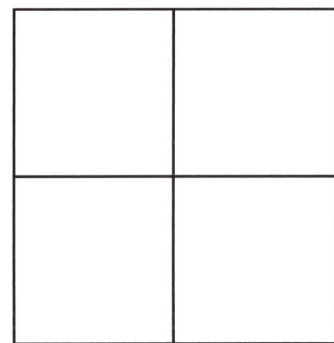

one half

Colour **one half** of each of these shapes in **three** different ways.

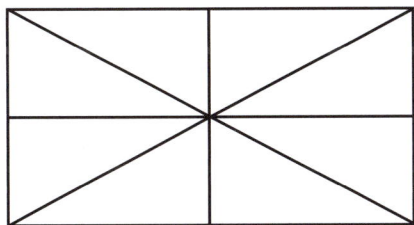

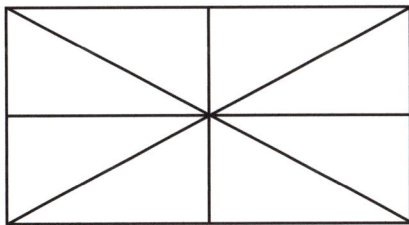

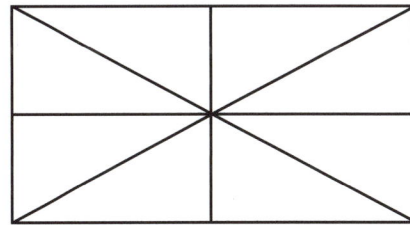

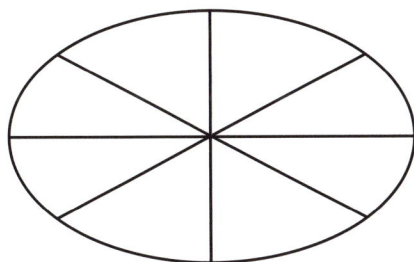

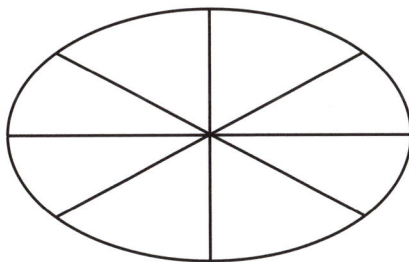

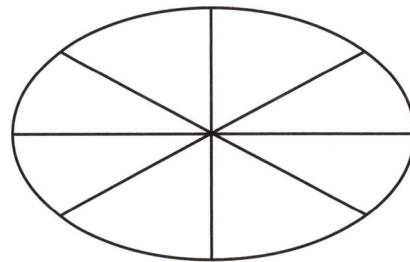

animal fractions

Circle the right amount for each group of animals.

one half

one quarter

one quarter

one half

Measurement

longest, tallest . . .

white
car

black
car

red
car

Which car is the longest?

Did you know?
Giraffes are the world's tallest mammals, thanks to their long legs and necks. A giraffe's legs alone are taller than many humans!

Gina

Gerald

Georgia

Gio

Which giraffe is the tallest?

caterpillar measuring

Compare the lengths of the caterpillars below.

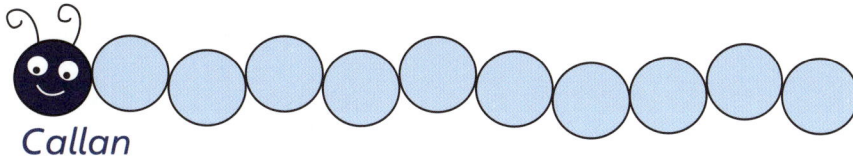

Callan

Chloe

Craig

Casey

Cathy

Circle the **longest** caterpillar in blue and the **shortest** caterpillar in green.

Which two caterpillars are the **same** length?

_____ and _____

Which caterpillar is **shorter**, Chloe or Craig? _____

Which caterpillar is **longer**, Casey or Cathy? _____

Draw a caterpillar **shorter** than Chloe.

colourful carrots

Use the squares to measure the carrots below.

Carrot **A**

Carrot **B**

Carrot **C**

Carrot **D**

Which is the **longest** carrot?

Which carrot is **shorter** than Carrot D, but **longer** than Carrot C?

How many squares long is the **shortest** carrot?

Which carrot is **double** the length of Carrot A?

Which carrot is **half** the length of Carrot D?

measuring mania

How long is the room you are in? How wide is it?

Pace off the length of the room, stepping carefully heel to toe. Count each step.

My room is ☐ paces long and ☐ paces wide.

Measure your dining table with your hands. Measure from the heel of your hand to the tip of your longest finger.

My table is ☐ handspans long and ☐ handspans wide.

We can also measure in **centimetres** with a **ruler**.

Look around your house for 5 things which measure **less** than 15cm, and 5 things which measure **more** than 15cm.

If you don't have a ruler, use the cutout ruler on page 383.

pencil power

Using a ruler measure the pencils below.

If you don't have a ruler, use the cutout ruler on page 383.

Which is the **longest** pencil?

How long is the **shortest** pencil?

Which two pencils are the **same** length?

and

Find six pens or pencils in your house and order them by size.

Using a ruler, draw lines in the boxes below to match the length.

3cm

5cm

6cm

2cm

14cm

10cm

9cm

weighty business

Which object is **heavier**? Circle the object that weighs **more**.

Cut out the animals on page 357. Arrange them below in order of **lightest** to **heaviest**.

Which animal on the previous page did you think would be the **lightest**? _____

Which animal would be **lighter** than the elephant but **heavier** than the dog? _____

Can you think of an animal that would be **heavier** than a robin but **lighter** than a cat? _____

Can you think of an animal that would be **lighter** than a robin? Draw it here.

Number these household objects in order of weight, with 6 the **heaviest** and 1 the **lightest**.

We weigh lighter things like these in **grams**.

We weigh heavier things like these in **kilograms**.

Draw lines from the objects to how you would weight them, either in **grams** or **kilograms**.

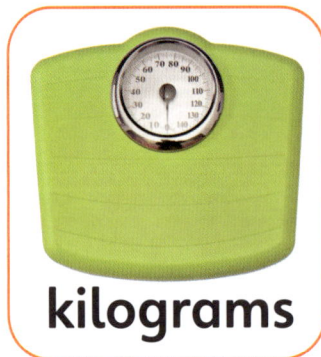

grams

kilograms

weighing up – biscuit recipe

Follow the recipe to make your own homemade biscuits.

ingredients

100g butter

150g plain flour

60g sugar

teaspoon icing sugar

equipment

kitchen scales

baking tray

mixing bowl

rolling pin

cookie cutters

You could try . . . replacing 20g of flour with 20g of cocoa powder to make chocolate shortbread biscuits.

Step 1

Heat the oven to 170C/gas 3. Work the mixture with your hands or a food processor until it looks like breadcrumbs, then squeeze together to form a dough.

Step 2

Place the dough on a clean, lightly floured surface, and roll out to $\frac{3}{4}$cm thickness.

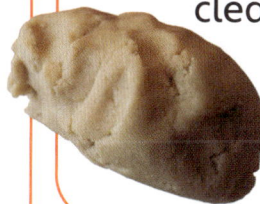

Step 3

Cut out shapes using the cutters.

Then place them on a lightly greased baking tray.

Ask an adult to help you with the oven.

Step 4

Bake for around 20-25 minutes, or until lightly golden in colour. Cool on a wire rack, then dust with icing sugar before eating!

These biscuits are delicious with a glass of cold milk!

empty or full

Join the label to the correct bottle. One bottle will have two labels!

half empty full nearly empty nearly full half full empty

glass **A** *glass* **B** *glass* **C** *glass* **D** *glass* **E** *glass* **F** *glass* **G**

Which glass is **empty**?

Which glass has **more than** glass G?

Which glass has **more than** glass E, but **less than** glass C?

empty or full

more or less?

Which item on the right holds more? Circle it.

Carry out your own experiment in a basin or sink. Find some of the things below. Use a mug to measure how much water each object can hold. Write your results below.

It takes ___ mugs to fill the jug.

It takes ___ mugs to fill the glass.

It takes ___ mugs to fill the pan.

It takes ___ mugs to fill the bowl.

It takes ___ mugs to fill the carton.

The object that holds the most water is the _____

Complete these sentences with **more than** or **less than**.

The pan holds _____ than the jug.

The glass holds _____ than the bowl.

The carton holds _____ than the pan.

If you have a funnel, it will make it easier!

measuring in ml

How much liquid is in each jug?

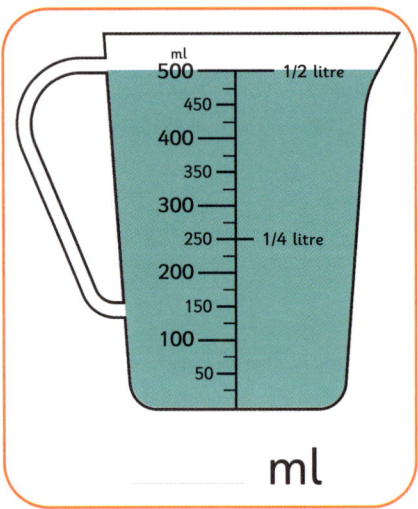

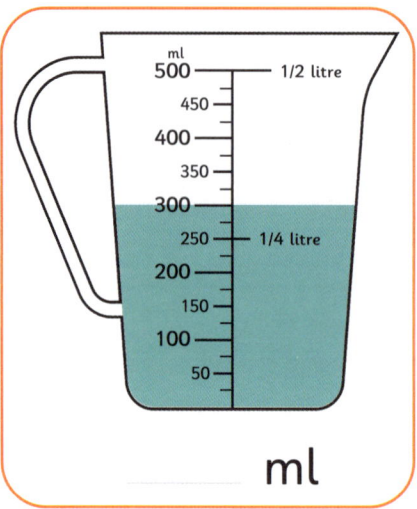

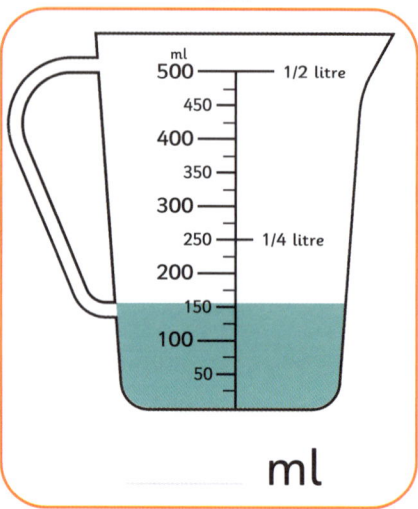

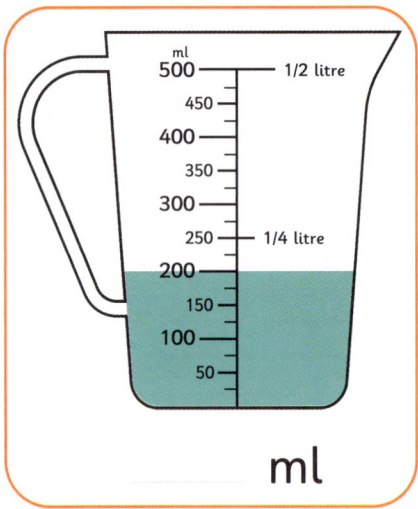

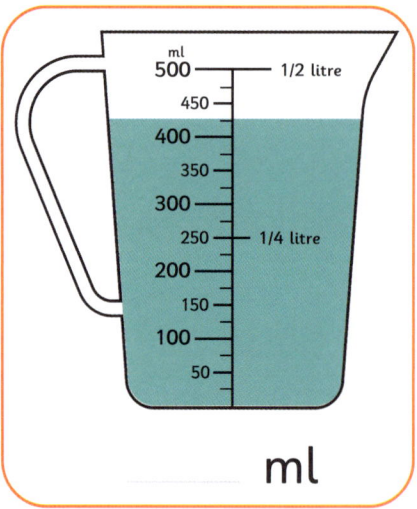

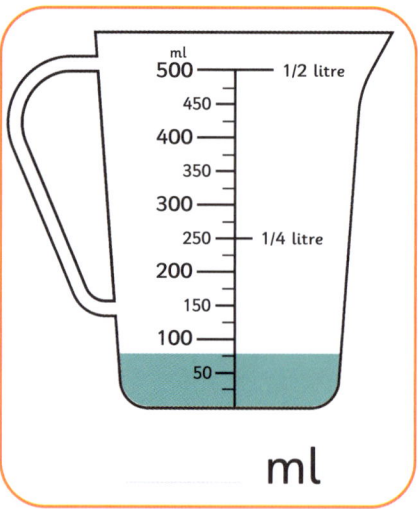

ml	ml	ml
ml	ml	ml

Colour each jug to match the quantity shown.

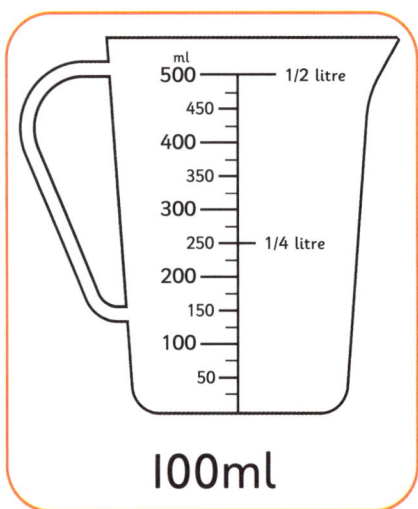

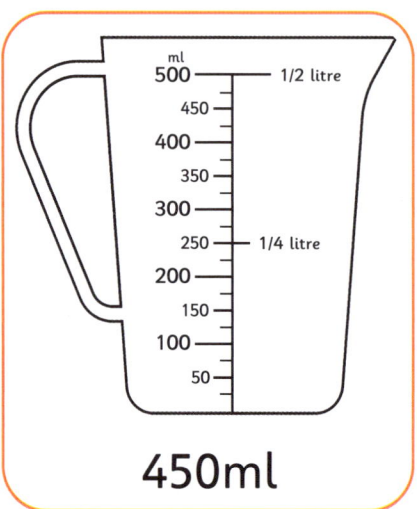

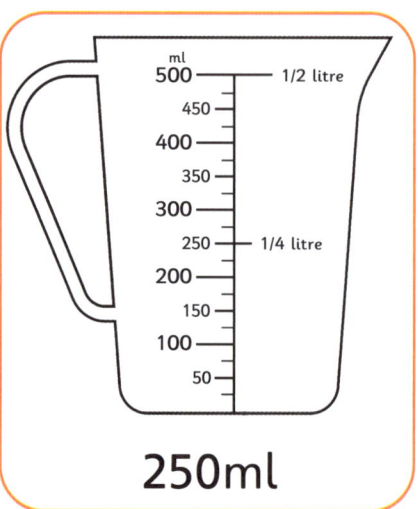

100ml	450ml	250ml

time sequencing

What is quicker . . . ? Circle the thing that is **quicker**.

What takes longer . . . ? Circle the answer.

Having dinner | Tying shoe laces

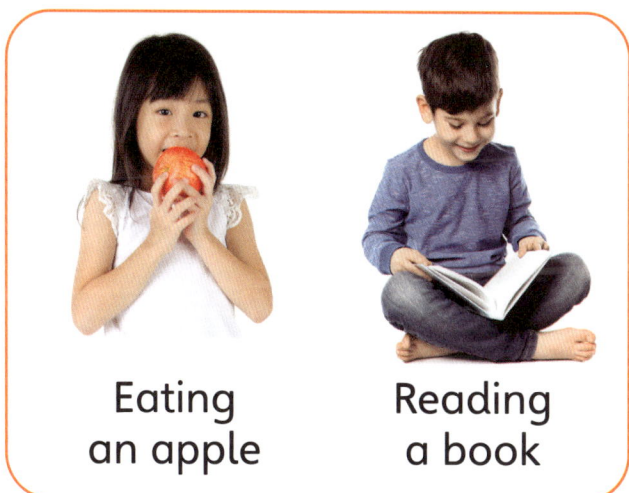

Eating an apple | Reading a book

What do you do first . . . ? Circle the answer.

Put toothpaste on your brush | Brush your teeth

Go cycling | Put on a helmet

What **order** do you do things in the morning? Label the pictures **1** to **6** in the order you do them.

Now write about your morning routine. Complete the sentences.

First, I _____

Then, I _____

Next, I _____

After that, I _____

Last of all, I _____

Then, I'm ready to _____

Can you think of anything else you do before school? Write it below. **When** do you do it?

Complete these sentences using one of the words below.

| before | morning | next | then | after | evening |
| afternoon | yesterday | tomorrow | first | today |

I put on my trainers _____ I go outside.

This _____ I woke up late.

We finish school in the _____ .

We eat dinner in the _____ .

I play with my friends _____ school.

We are going on holiday _____ week.

I can't play today, but I will be able to _____ .

We have dinner _____ we wash up.

I can't go to school _____ , because I'm poorly.

It snowed _____ , so today I'll make a snowman.

The _____ thing I do in the morning is stretch!

days and months

Fill the months in below in the correct order.
The first is done for you.

January

December	May	July	October
February	March	June	September
January	August	April	November

Can you find all the months of the year in the word-search below? Circle each word when you find it.

b	j	t	j	u	l	y	w	u	i	m	p
a	a	a	p	r	i	l	d	g	j	k	n
c	n	y	d	e	c	e	m	b	e	r	o
e	u	a	f	e	b	r	u	a	r	y	v
r	a	u	w	m	e	v	c	b	n	m	e
m	r	g	x	a	r	j	u	n	e	o	m
a	y	u	q	y	r	a	y	u	i	n	b
r	r	s	h	o	c	t	o	b	e	r	e
c	s	t	j	g	l	b	l	o	s	p	r
h	c	s	e	p	t	e	m	b	e	r	t

Answer these questions.

Which month comes after October? _____

Which month is between May and July? _____

Which two months begin with A?

_____ and _____

Which month does May come after? _____

Cut out the days of the week on page 373, and stick them below in the correct order, starting with Monday.

Answer these questions.

Which two days begin with T?

_____

_____

Which day comes after Friday?

_____

Write the day to fill in the missing labels.

Yesterday	Today	Tomorrow
	Saturday	
	Thursday	
	Tuesday	

my calendar

Cut out the pieces on pages 365–369 and make your own calendar on the reverse side of this page by attaching the labels with reusable adhesive. You can tear this page out and pin it up. Keep the cut out labels safe by storing them in an envelope or box so that you can reuse them.

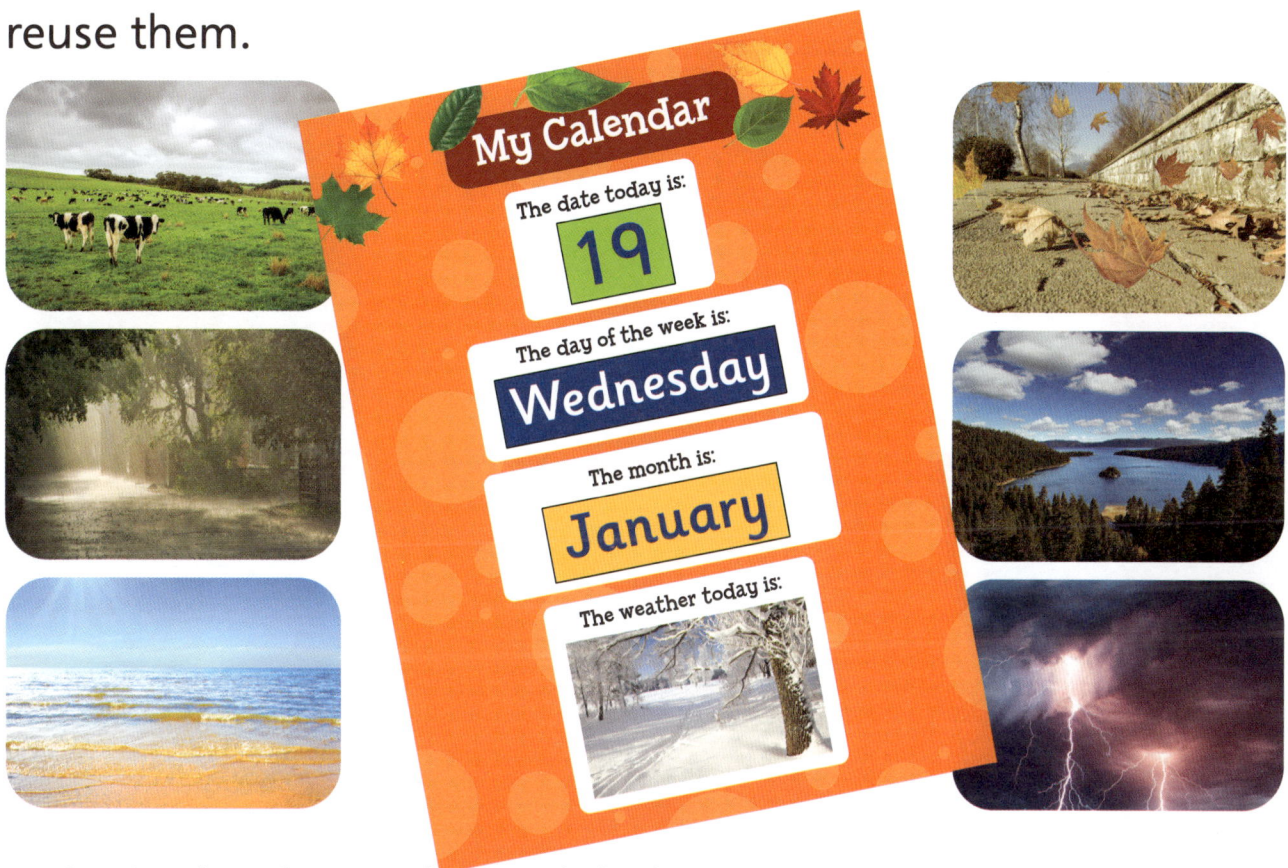

Calendar

My Calendar

The date today is:

19

The day of the week is:

Wednesday

The month is:

January

The weather today is:

Write in the day and month below.

My birthday is on

My Calendar

The date today is:

The day of the week is:

The month is:

The weather today is:

hours, minutes and seconds

60 seconds = 1 minute	60 minutes = 1 hour	24 hours = 1 day	7 days = 1 week	52 weeks = 1 year

How long does it take to . . . ?
Join the activities up to the most appropriate time.

watch a programme

do 20 star jumps

yawn

go for a bike ride

play football

1 minute

1 hour

1 second

tie your laces

eat an apple

clap once

blow out a candle

play a game

skip 10 times

smile

get undressed

How many times do you think you can do each activity below in a minute? Use a clock or watch to time yourself.

Activity	Guess	Count
 count to 10	☐	☐
 clap	☐	☐
 star jumps	☐	☐
write your name	☐	☐

telling the time

!

The long hand is the **minute hand**.

The short hand is the **hour hand**.

This clock shows **five o'clock**, or **5:00**.

When the minute hand points to 6 it is **half past** the hour.

When the minute hand points to 12 it is **o'clock**.

This clock shows **half past three**, or **3:30**.

What time does each clock show?

Circle the clock which shows the correct time.

 Feeding time at the zoo is at 3.30.

The plane departs at 8.30.

Draw the correct time on each clock.

8 o'clock

half past 9

12 o'clock

half past 11

3 o'clock

half past 6

Write the time shown on each clock. Then draw a picture of what you might be doing at that time.

in the morning

in the afternoon

in the evening

at night

clock bingo

Cut out the clocks on page 371, then put them in a pile, face down. Choose one of the bingo cards below. Take turns with a friend to pick a clock card and match it to the time on your bingo card. If it doesn't match, put it back. The first one to cover all their times is the winner!

half past 3	9 o'clock	half past 6	half past 11
2 o'clock	half past 5	4 o'clock	half past 8

1 o'clock	half past 7	half past 10	6 o'clock
half past 4	8 o'clock	half past 2	half past 9

money matters

Match the coins and notes to their value.

5p	50p	£2	£20	1p	£1

20p	£10	10p	2p	£5

Cut out the coins on page 373 and place them below in order of value, from lowest to highest.

How much money is in each purse or wallet?

Alonso's wallet

Gina's purse

Ahmed's wallet

Aisha's purse

Zach's wallet

Becky's purse

Toys are on sale at the local shop. Which toy can each child can afford to buy with their money? Colour in red the label of the toy he or she can buy.

Alonso

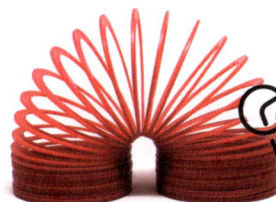
10p 20p

Gina

5p 8p

Ahmed

20p 25p

Aisha

15p 12p

Zach

20p 15p

Becky

18p 20p

Count how much the coins are worth. How much extra do you need to buy each toy? Draw more 1p and 2p coins to make up the total.

14p

10p

8p

5p

7p

12p

money problems

1 Maria has 12p.
Each sweet costs 2p.
How many sweets
can she buy?

2 Zach and Rob have been saving
up to buy a robot dog. They
have £9 between them. The
dog costs £12. How much more
money do they need?

3 Jilly takes 20p to the cake
sale. She spends half her
money. How much does
she have left?

4 Jordan has 20p. Pens are 10p and pencils are 5p.

How many pens can Jordan buy?

How many pencils can he buy
with the same money?

5 Izzy takes £5 to a car boot sale. She spends £2 on a hat and £1 on a bracelet. How much change should she get?

6 Apples and oranges are 10p each.

How much would 5 apples be?

How much would 1 apple and 3 oranges be?

7 Kai counts his money. He has two 50p coins. Which toy can he afford? Circle the toy.

£1

£2

8 Libby buys two cornflake cakes and one cupcake.

£1

£2

How much has she spent?

If she gave the shopkeeper £5, how much change will she get?

Geometry

2D shapes

Colour in the shapes below and complete the information for the fact files.

Number of sides [ ]

Name

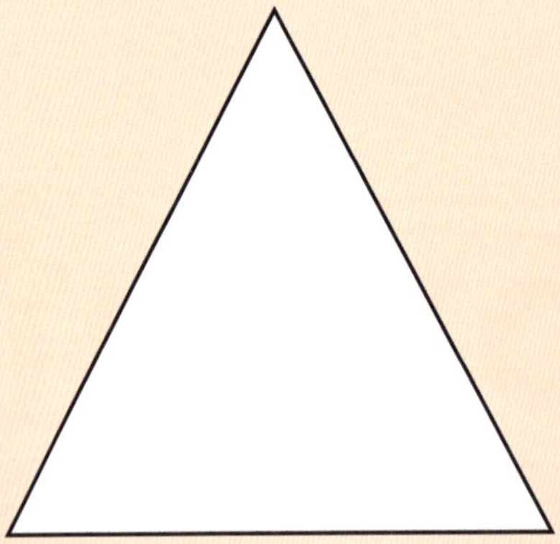

_____

Number of sides [ ]

Name

_____

Number of sides [ ]

Name

_____

Number of sides [ ]

Name

_____

Number of sides [ ]

Name

_____

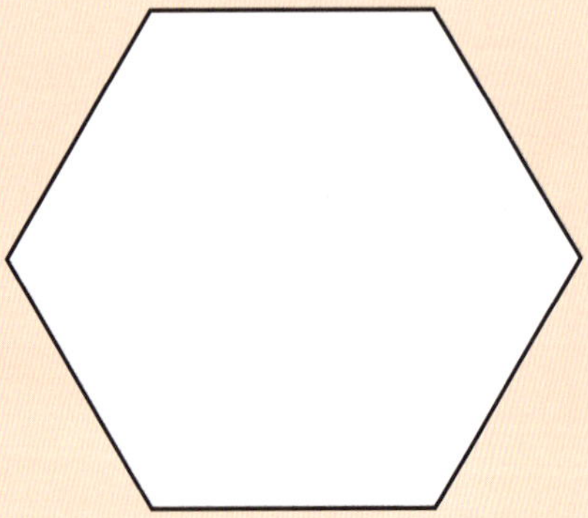

Number of sides [ ]

Name

_____

rectangle   hexagon   square   triangle   pentagon   circle

How many of each shape can you see below?

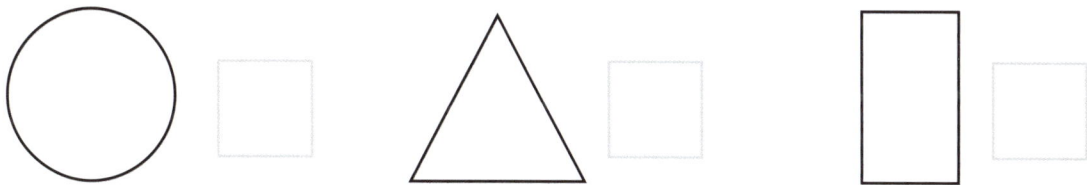

Which shape appears **most**? _____

Name three common objects that are **rectangular**.

_____

3D shapes

Cut out the 3D shapes on page 375 and stick them into the correct box.

pyramid	**sphere**	**cylinder**
cone	**triangular prism**	**cuboid**

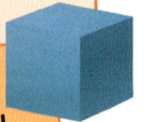

Fill in the venn diagram.

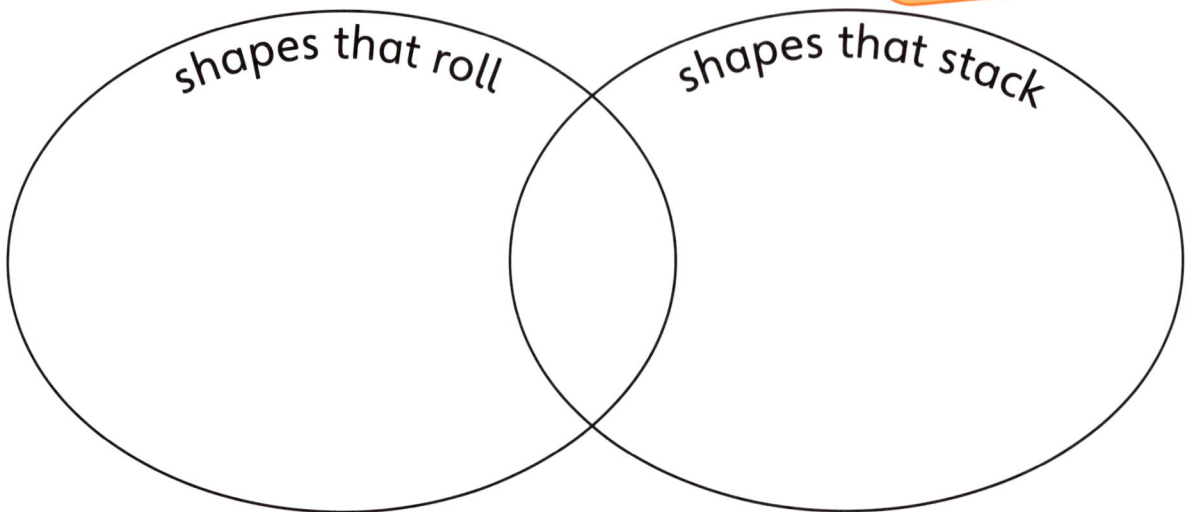

A cube is a square cuboid.

shapes that roll   shapes that stack

building with 3D shapes

Colour in the 3D man using the key below.

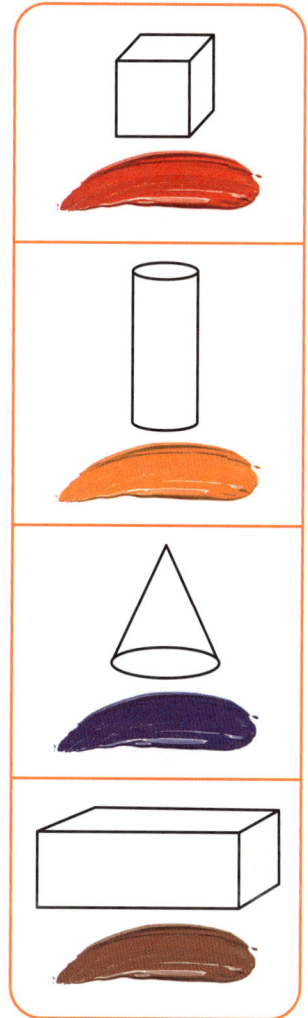

How many of each solid shape are used to make the figure?

Everyday objects can resemble 3D shapes. Cut out the objects on page 377 and place them in the correct category.

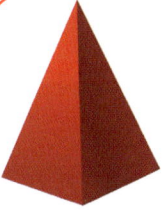

shape hunt

Look for **3D** shapes around your house and garden. Draw some of the objects you find. Were there some you couldn't find? Which were they?

shape patterns

Cut out the **3D shapes** on page 373, then use them to complete the repeating patterns below.

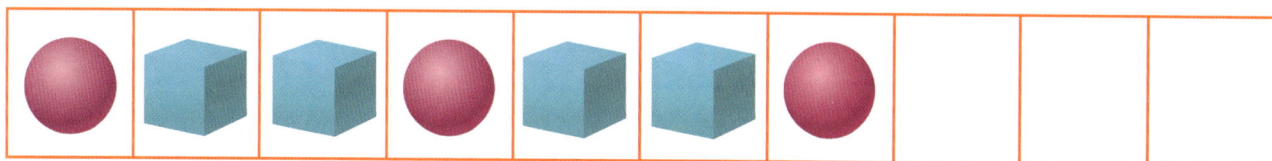

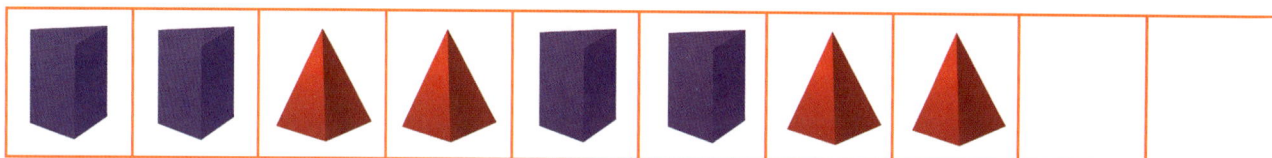

Draw your own repeating **2D shape** patterns below.

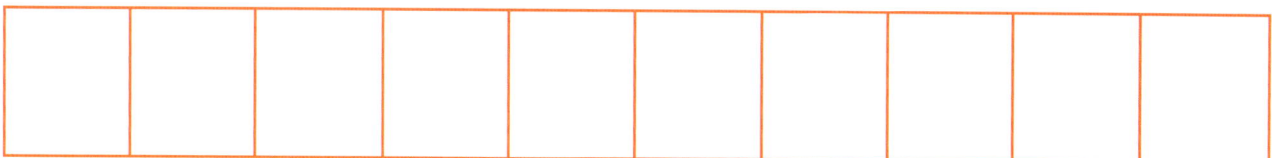

position

Each picture shows a different position. Write the correct position below each picture, choosing from the words below.

behind **under** **in front of** **on**

above **in** **between** **next to**

Look at the pictures below. Is each animal facing **left** or **right**? Write the answer below.

Follow the instructions in each box.

Draw a circle to the **left** of the square.

Draw a triangle to the **right** of the circle.

Draw a fork to the **left** of the knife.

Draw a tree to the **right** of the house.

Following the instructions in each box.

Colour the **top** square blue, the **middle** square green, and the **bottom** square red.

Draw **dots** around the **outside** of the circle. Draw a **square** in the **middle** of the circle.

How many ways can you describe the position of the £1 coin? Use words such as **below, above, to the left or right of, between**, and so on.

Write some of the ways below.

The £1 coin is . . .

Read the clues below and fill in the missing names. Then answer the questions.

Jinny

Ben

Jinny is directly **above** Sam.

Fifi is to the **left** of Jinny.

Kai is to the **left** of Lily.

Dan is to the **right** of Jinny.

Lily is directly **below** Sam.

May is directly **above** Ben.

Kieran is directly **below** Fifi.

Who is in the **middle**? _____

Who is directly **below** Dan? _____

| quarter turn clockwise | half turn | three-quarter turn clockwise | full turn |

Cut out the monsters on page 379, and stick them in the correct positions below.

Starting position	Quarter turn clockwise	Half turn clockwise	Three-quarter turn clockwise	Full turn clockwise

Look at the grid below. Keep track of which direction you are facing.

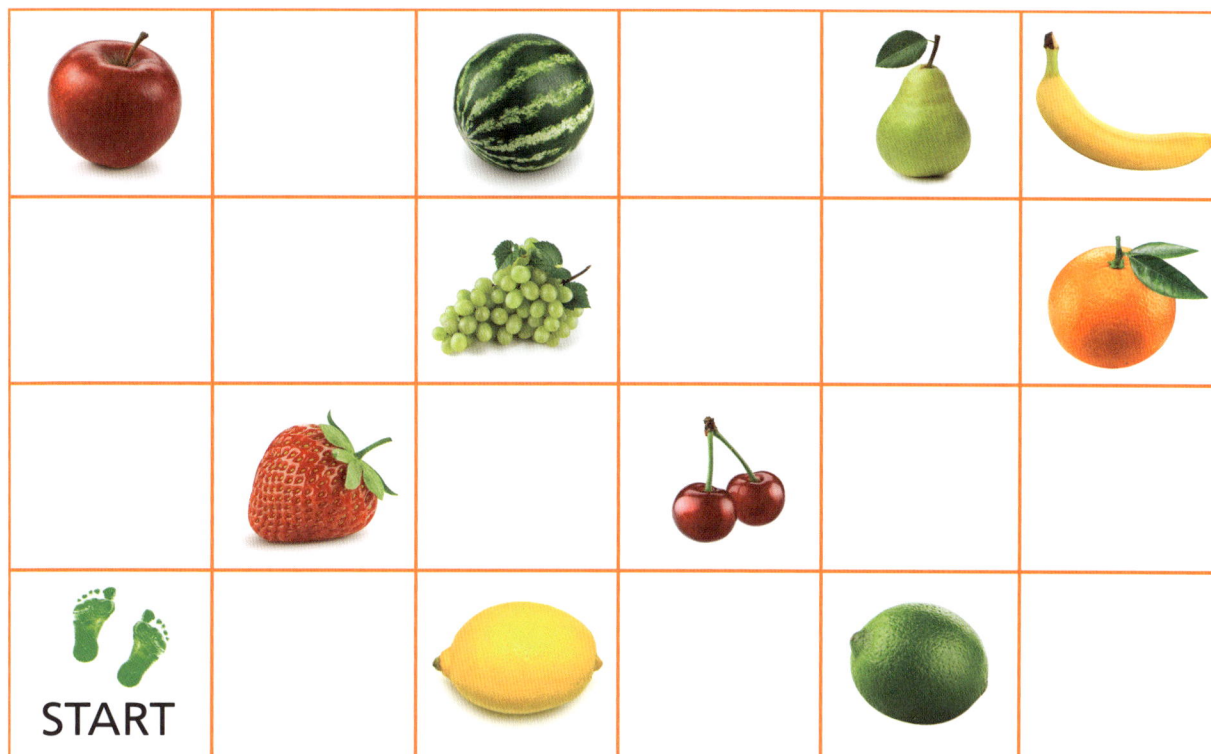

🍎		🍉		🍐	🍌
		🍇			🍊
	🍓		🍒		
START		🍋		🟢	

From the start, move forwards 3 squares. What fruit is in the square? _____

Make a right turn. Move forwards 5 squares. What fruit is in the square? _____

Make a half turn. Move forwards I square. What fruit is in the square? _____

Move forwards 2 squares. Make a left turn. Move forwards I square. What fruit is in the square? _____

Describe how to get to the lemon from where you are.

_____

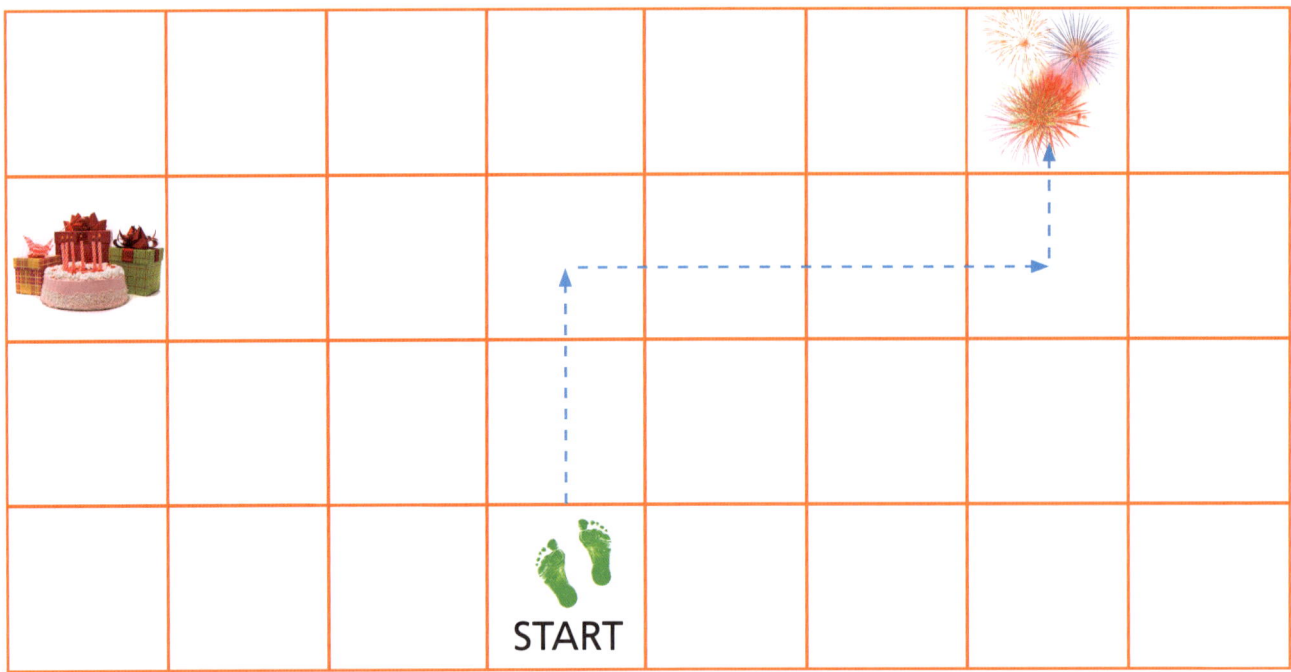

Describe how to get to the **fireworks**, following the blue path.

First, move forwards ☐ squares.

Then, turn _____ . Move forwards ☐ squares.

Turn _____ . Move forwards ☐ squares.

Now draw your own route to the **party** on the grid above, and describe how to get there.

Science

trees

Trees are plants. All plants have parts. Each part helps the plant live and grow.

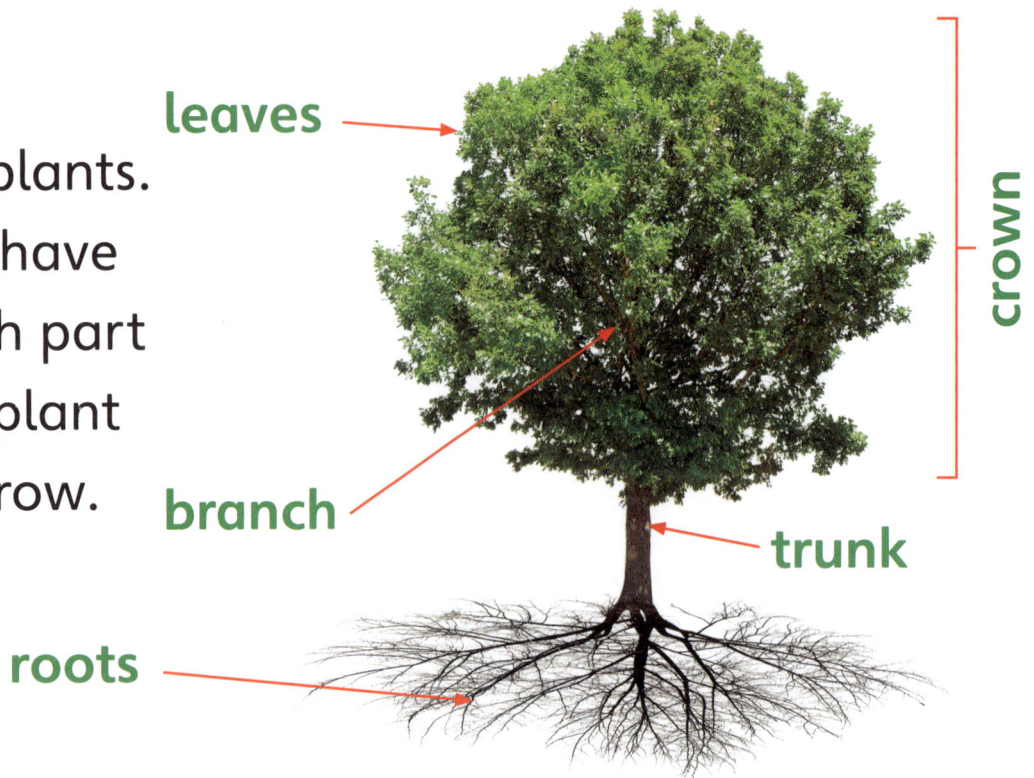

leaves

crown

branch

trunk

roots

Read the clues below, then say what each part is.

We spread underground. We take in water and support the tree. We are _____ .

We grow on branches and are often green. We use sunlight to make food. We are _____ .

I am strong and firm and hold up the tree. I am protected by bark. I am the _____ .

We grow from the trunk and split into smaller parts. We are _____ .

I am the whole of the top of the tree. I am the _____ .

deciduous trees

Deciduous trees shed their leaves in the autumn. Draw lines to match these deciduous trees to their leaves.

English oak

horse chestnut

willow

horse chestnut

willow

European ash

birch

English oak

lime

birch

European ash

lime

Did you know?
Evergreen trees are trees that have leaves all year round. Many – such as spruce, fir and pine trees – have needles instead of broad leaves.

269

types of plants

! There are many different types of plants, from grass to tall trees, from roses to ferns. While different in some ways, in others they will be similar.

Some plants have flowers, some don't. Which of these plants have flowers? Circle those that do.

grass

pansies

tulips

ivy

Some plants need lots of sunshine. Others prefer shade. Circle the plants that need lots of sunshine.

sunflower

moss

ferns

orange tree

Did you know?
Weeds are just wild plants that grow where they aren't wanted!

plants homes

! Plants grow in different places, from the hot dry desert to the bottom of the sea! Over time they change to adapt to where they live.

Some plants live in or beside water. Others need very little water at all to survive. Circle the plant that needs hardly any water.

water lilies

cacti

reeds

Cut out the plants on page 375 and stick them in the correct place.

desert

meadow

forest

water

how plants grow

All plants begin as seeds. Most seeds need soil to grow, as well as water and sunlight.

Sprouts then become young plants called **seedlings**.

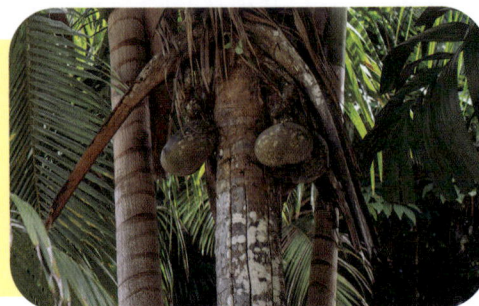

grow your own bean plant

What you need:

- beans (e.g. broad beans)
- spray bottle (optional)
- soil (for later)
- paper towels
- jar
- water

What you do:

1. Fold some paper towels and dampen them slightly.
2. Put the paper towels around the inside of the jar.
3. Put one or two more damp paper towels into the bottom of the jar.

4. Put a few beans between the paper towels and the jar.

5. Check every day. Spray water into the jar if the paper towels get dry.

6. When leaves come out, make sure that the jar is in a sunny place.

7. Place in a warm spot but not in direct sunlight.

8. Add water when the paper towels get dry.

What happens next: In a few days, your bean should sprout **roots**. Next, its first **leaves** will come out.

leaves

stem

roots

sprout

As the plant grows, the roots will spread downward. The **stem** will grow upward. More leaves will grow.

After about two weeks, your plant will need **soil**. Plant it in a pot and watch it grow!

a flowering plant

Write the labels in the correct place to complete the diagram of a flowering plant.

stem

bud

flower

leaves

roots

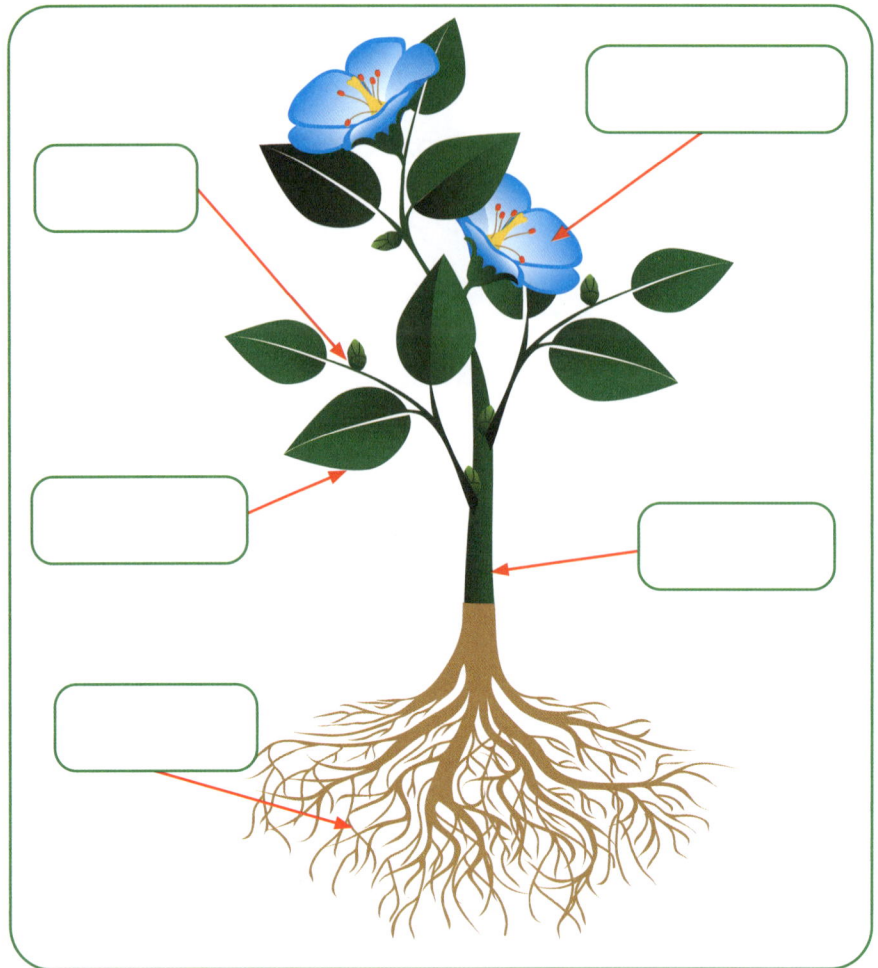

Now draw and label your own flowering plant in the pot.

plants as food

We eat lots of plants, but we don't always eat the same part of the plant.

root carrots
bulb beetroot
leaves cabbage
fruit strawberries
tuber potatoes
stem celery
flower cauliflower
seeds corn

Join the fruit or vegetable to the correct part of the plant.

broccoli

corn

potatoes

fruit stem
tuber root
seeds flower
bulb leaves

lettuce

carrot

onion

strawberries

celery

through the seasons

Depending on the time of year, plants can look very different. Draw lines to match each tree to the correct season.

spring	summer	autumn	winter

Write one sentence about plants in each season. Use the pictures for ideas.

 In spring _____

_____

 In summer _____

_____

 In autumn _____

_____

 In winter _____

_____

plant hunt

How many of these plants can you find in your garden or near where you live?

Some of these plants can only be spotted in certain seasons.

oak tree

ivy

daisy

horse chestnut tree

grass

tulip

birch tree

moss

geranium

fir tree

snowdrop

sunflower

cherry tree

dandelion

pansy

ferns

buttercup

rose

animals — mammals

Humans are mammals!

Animals can be sorted into different groups depending on their characteristics.

❗ **Mammals** are **warm-blooded** animals with **fur** or **hair**. They have a backbone or **spine**. They give birth to **live babies**, which are then fed on their mother's **milk**.

Draw lines to join the mammals to where they live.

dolphin

cat

Did you know?
Bats are the only mammals that can truly fly, although flying squirrels are great gliders!

sheep

air

bat

land

dog

water

monkey

meerkat

bear

fox

killer whale

mouse

Did you know?
Whales and dolphins might look like large fish, but they are mammals! They give birth to live young and feed them milk. They don't have gills.

What is your favourite mammal? Draw a picture of it. Label it using some of the words below.

nose fin eye mouth head wing
leg tail paw hoof ear fur

Why do you like this animal?

_____

_____

birds and reptiles

! A **bird** is a type of animal that has **feathers**, **wings** and a **beak**. All birds **lay eggs**.

Look at the diagram of the house sparrow. Write your own labels on the picture of the parrot.

beak

wings

feathers

tail

claws

! **Reptiles** are **cold-blooded** animals that have **scales**. They also **lay eggs**.

Here are some examples of reptile scales. Colour in the scales on the right with your own pattern.

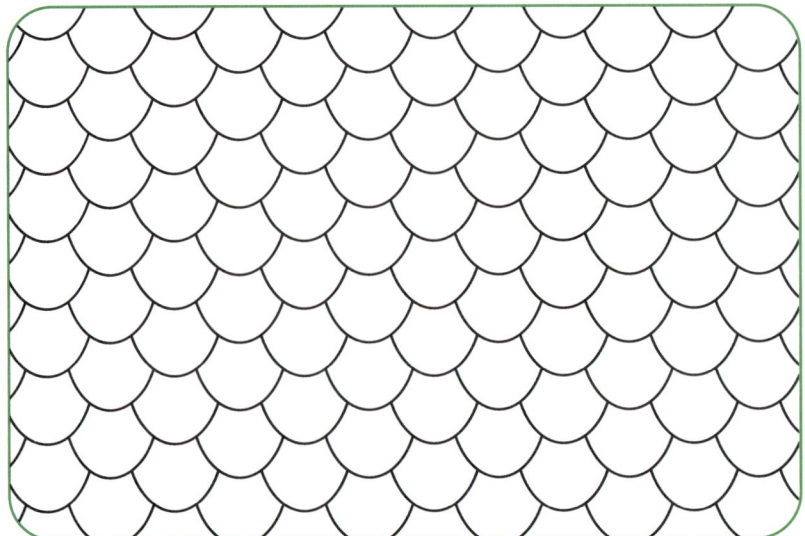

Circle in blue the animals that are **birds**. Circle in green the animals that are **reptiles**.

alligator

budgie

chameleon

duck

lizard

tortoise

eagle

crocodile

chicken

ostrich

penguin

owl

snake

iguana

Did you know?
Reptiles and birds might be very different, but they also share some things in common, such as laying eggs. Most birds also have reptile-like scales on their legs and feet.

fish and amphibians

Fish are **cold-blooded** animals which **live in water** and have **gills.**

Look at the diagram below. Then draw and colour your own coral reef fish, and add labels.

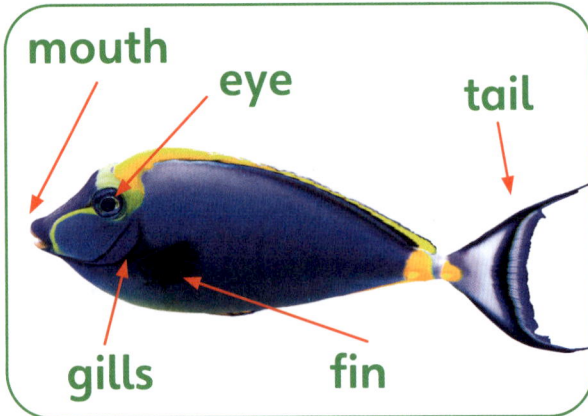

mouth

eye

tail

gills fin

Amphibians are also **cold-blooded.** They **live partly in water and partly on land.** They hatch from **eggs.**

Look at the diagram below. Then say whether each statement is true or false by circling the answer.

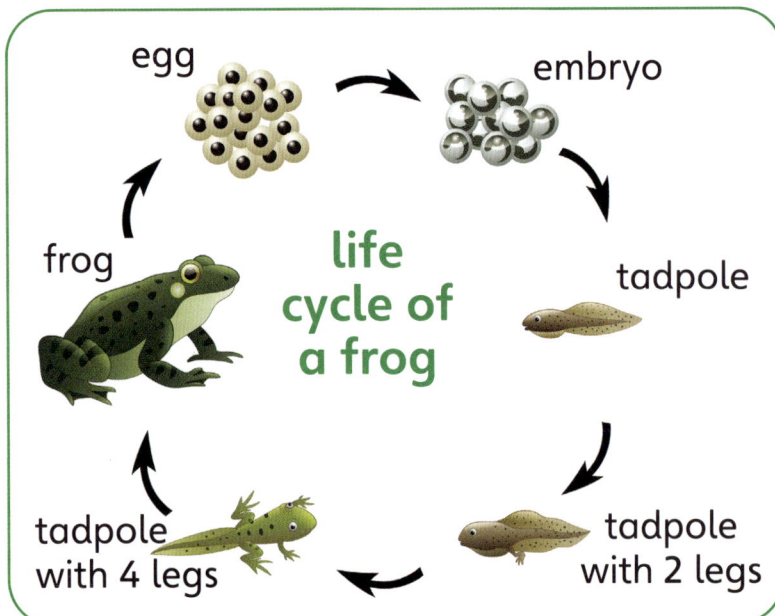

egg embryo

frog life cycle of a frog

tadpole

tadpole with 4 legs tadpole with 2 legs

Tadpoles are the same shape as an adult frog.

true   *false*

Tadpoles always have 4 legs.

true   *false*

How many fish and amphibians can you count?

frog

newt

goldfish

tuna

salmon

dart frog

yellow tang

cod

shark

toad

eel

marlin

salamander

roach

tree frog

royal angelfish

Fish ☐   Amphibians ☐

who's who?

Cut out the animals on pages 381 and 383 and stick them below and on the next page, placing them in the correct category.

mammals

Did you know?
The duck-billed platypus, found only in Australia, is one of only two mammals that lays eggs. It is also the only mammal with a bill.

birds

reptiles

fish

amphibians

same but different

Compare each pair of animals below. Say what is the same, and what is different. Use some of the words at the bottom of the next page.

tortoise

tiger

shark

pig

owl

snake

cat

frog

beak water eyes mouth land wings

scales tail air fins legs ears fur

animal guessing game

Draw a line to match the animal to the clue.

? I am the largest land **mammal**. I have big ears and a very long nose that is called a trunk.

rattlesnake

? I am an **amphibian**. I can leap and swim, and have large, bulging eyes.

goldfish

? I am a **bird** and I am awake at night. I make a hooting sound.

frog

? I am a **fish** and am orangey-gold in colour. Some people keep me as a pet.

owl

? I am a **reptile** and slither on the ground. I have a rattle at the tip of my tail.

elephant

? I am a **bird** but I can't fly. I have black and white feathers and webbed feet.

? I am a **reptile** and can change the colour of my skin. My eyes can move in two different directions at once.

? I am a **fish**. I have an extremely long, flat, pointed bill which gives me my name.

? I am an **amphibian**. I look like a frog, but my skin is rough, and I prefer to crawl, not leap.

? I am a **mammal** and I live on a farm. People like to use my wool to make clothes.

swordfish

toad

penguin

chameleon

sheep

animal parts

Look at the diagrams below for each animal. Then answer the questions.

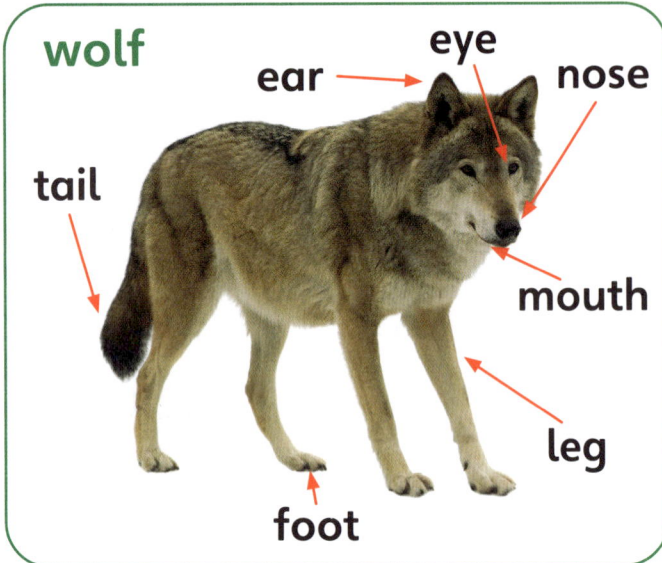

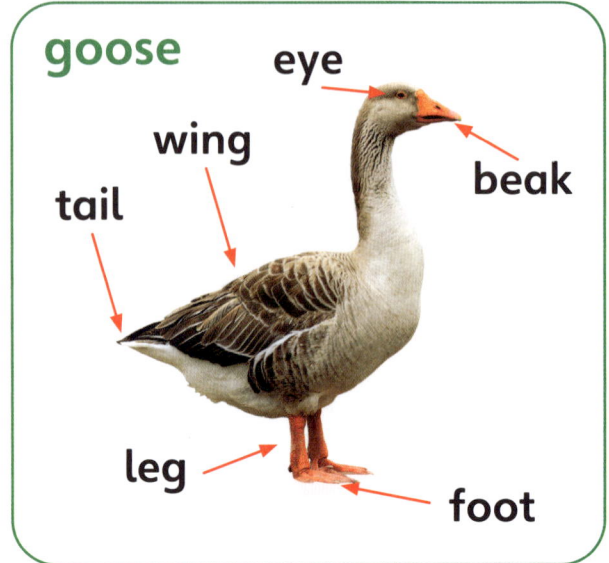

wolf

ear → eye nose
tail
mouth
leg
foot

goose

eye
wing
tail
beak
leg
foot

❶ What parts does the wolf use to move?

❷ What part does the goose use to swim?

shark

fin tail
nose eye
mouth gills fin

❸ What parts does the shark use to swim?

❹ What parts doesn't the shark have that the others do?

❺ What parts do all three animals have?

what do animals eat

Koalas are **herbivores** – they only eat **plants**.

Lions are **carnivores** – they only eat other **animals**.

Most bears are **omnivores** – they eat both **plants** and **animals**.

Draw a line to join each animal to the food it eats.

animal

shark

giant panda

squirrel

cow

robin

tortoise

cheetah

what they eat

fish

leaves

grass

acorn

worm

bamboo

spring-bok

the human body

Cut out the labels on page 379 and put them in the right places.

Did you know?
More than half of your body is made up of water.

the human body

senses

! People and animals have five **senses**. We **see** with our eyes. We **hear** with our ears. We **smell** with our nose. We **taste** with our mouth. We **touch** with our skin.

Write your own labels for the five senses.

Join the senses up to the correct picture.

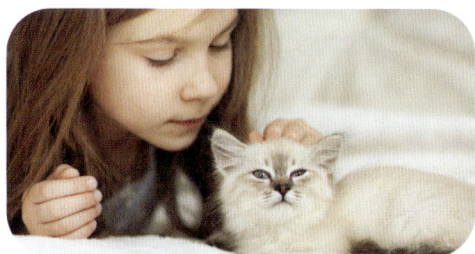

sight

taste

hearing

smell

touch

sensory scavenger hunt

Take a sensory trip around your house and garden. See if you can find three things for each sense category. Draw a picture of each thing you find.

Things I **saw**.

Things I **heard**.

Things I **smelt**.

Things I **felt**.

Things I **tasted**.

Don't taste anything that isn't safe to eat!

keeping healthy

There are lots of things we can do to keep healthy.

eat healthy food

exercise

keep clean

Circle the types of **exercise** that you like to do.

Is there anything else you like to do? _____

Colour in the stars for the **food** that is **healthy**.

materials

The objects around us are made from different materials.

metal storage unit

bamboo supports

wooden fence

Join each object to the material it is made of.

wood   **plastic**   **metal**   **clay**   **rock**   **brick**

brick
house

metal
frame

glass
greenhouse

clay
pots

plastic
netting

Join each object to the material it is made of.

glass paper fabric rubber ceramic

Materials are chosen for their different properties.

This **rubber** hose is **flexible**.

It can bend easily to let you move around and reach all the areas of your outdoor space.

Circle the items below which are **flexible**.

Circle the items below which are **hard**.

What star quality does each of these items have?
Circle the property that best matches the material,
then explain why it is used.

waterproof   soft

_____

_____

waterproof   transparent

_____

_____

soft   hard

_____

_____

flexible   hard

_____

_____

Which of these objects is the odd one out and why?

1

The _____ is the odd one out because

_____

2

The _____ is the odd one out because

_____

3

The _____ is the odd one out because

_____

4

The _____ is the odd one out because

_____

Imagine you are designing a brand new toy. Decide what material – or materials – you will use. Will it be soft or hard, shiny or dull, flexible or stiff . . . ?

Draw your toy below.

Explain what the toy does and why you chose the materials that you did.

how strong is it?

Strength is a property of materials. Test the strength of different materials with this experiment.

What you need:

- 2 cans or beakers the same size
- paper, tinfoil, and cardboard
- 10 or more pennies
- ruler
- scissors

If you don't have enough pennies, use Lego bricks, or something else small.

What you do:

1. Cut out a strip of each material 5cm wide and 20cm long.

2. Set the cans or beakers 5cm apart on a flat surface.

3. Place a strip across the top so that an equal length of strip rests on each can or beaker.

4. Carefully place one penny at a time in the middle of the strip over the area between the cans, until the strip falls or breaks.

5. Count and record the number of pennies the material held before breaking.

6. Repeat for the other materials.

Record your **results** below.

Material	Number of pennies

Which material held the **most** pennies?

Which material held the **fewest**?

Which material was the **strongest**?

Which material was the **weakest**?

What happens when you use more than one piece of paper? Record your results above.

Try using a different material and record the results. You could try dried pasta or paper index cards!

how absorbent is it?

Absorption is another property of materials. Which materials absorb (soak up) water? Which materials do not? Which materials soak up the most water?

What you need:

- 4 (or more) equal-sized plates
- 4 (or more) equal-sized cups
- paper towel
- notebook paper
- flannel
- sponge
- other materials such as tinfoil, cotton balls, greaseproof paper
- water

What you do:

1. Pour the same amount of water onto each plate.

2. Place the first material onto a plate. Count to 40.

3. Take the material out and squeeze out the water into a cup. Label the cup.

4. Repeat for each material.

Results:

Compare the amount of water in the cups.
Which material absorbed the **most** water?

_____

Which material absorbed the **most** water?

_____

Label the objects below from **most absorbent** [1]
to **least absorbent** [4].

Materials that do **not** absorb water are **waterproof**.

What clothing do you have that is waterproof?

_____

Name something else that is waterproof.

_____

materials scavenger hunt

Look around your house and garden. See if you can find three things for each property. Draw a picture of each thing you find.

Something **hard**.

Something **soft**.

Something **flexible**.

Something **transparent**.

Something **waterproof**.

seasons

Spring in the UK is from March to May. There are lots of sudden rain showers, but the days begin to get warmer.

Summer in the UK is from June to August. It is the warmest season, with long sunny days and occasional thunderstorms.

Autumn in the UK is from September to November. It can be mild and dry, or wet and windy, and becomes colder.

Winter in the UK is from December to February. It is usually wet, windy and cold, with frost and even snow.

What do you associate with each season? Draw lines to match the pictures to the season.

spring **summer** **autumn** **winter**

What is your favourite season and what do you like to do in it? Draw a picture to show something you like to do.

What words do you associate with each season? Choose from the word bank, and add your own words. Each word can be used more than once.

fog   snow   hot   frost   rain   windy   warm

showery   icy   wet   dry   hail   sunny

breezy   cold   rainbow   cloudy   warm   stormy

spring

summer

autumn

winter

SCIENCE

Complete the sentences by filling in the missing word from the box below.

leaves days warmer bonfires ice cream cocoa
lambs gloves beach snowmen blossom colder

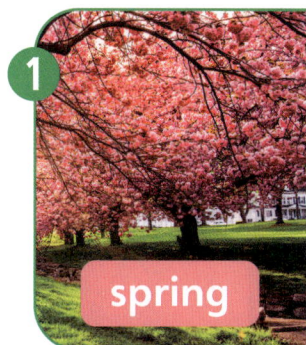

1 spring

The trees are covered with _____ .

The weather gets _____ .

Newborn _____ are in the fields.

2 summer

It is fun to eat _____ .

We make sandcastles on the _____ .

The _____ are long.

3 autumn

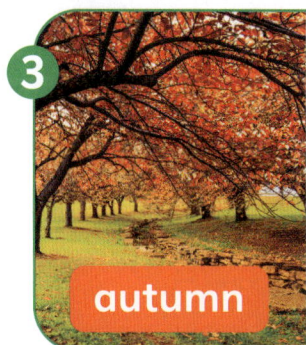

The _____ change colour.

The weather gets _____ .

We smell smoke from _____ .

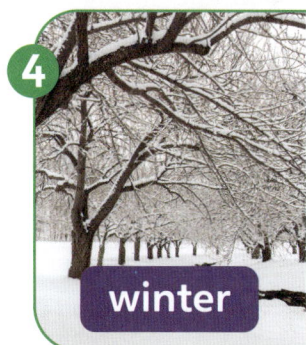

4 winter

People wear warm hats and _____ .

Children make _____ .

It's nice to drink hot _____ .

the sun in the sky

! The Earth is a planet. It spins around an invisible line, its **axis**, once every 24 hours. The Sun shines on different parts of the Earth as it rotates. It is **day** when the part of the Earth where you live **faces** the Sun. It is **night** when your side **faces away** from the Sun.

Label the diagram to show on which side of the Earth it is **day** or **night**.

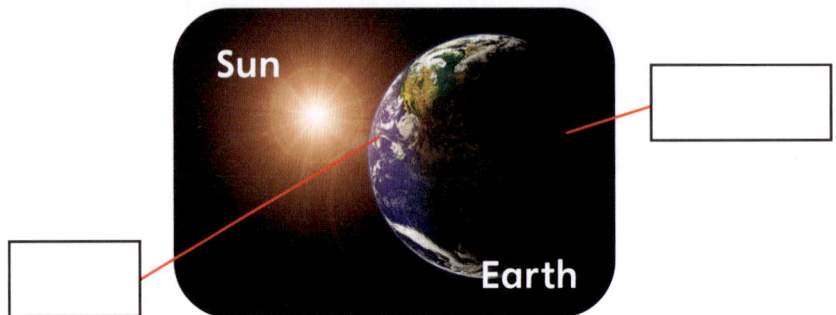

Sun

Earth

The Sun rises in the **east** and sets in the **west**. In the middle of the day, it appears directly overhead.

sunrise

noon

sunset

Never look directly at the Sun – even if you are wearing sunglasses!

Circle the answers.

How does the Sun move across the sky?

from east to west　　　　*from west to east*

Where is the Sun at noon?

in the ocean　　*directly overhead*　　*in the north*

Draw a picture of yourself at night, and a picture of yourself during the day.

> ❗ It takes the Earth one year to travel round the Sun. Because the Earth is tilted, this causes our **seasons**, and changes the length of **day** and **night**.

In **summer, days are longer** because our part of the planet is **tilted towards** the **Sun**. In **winter, days are shorter**, because we are **tilted away** from the **Sun**.

Circle the answers.

What season is it when the Earth is tilted towards the Sun?

summer   *winter*

Are winter days longer or shorter?

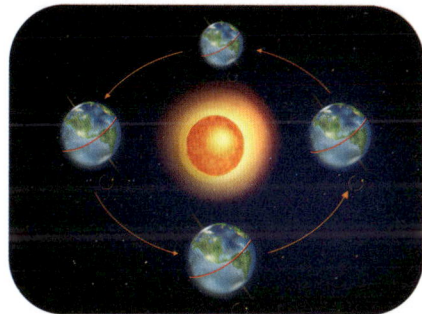

longer   *shorter*

Did you know?
Seasons are opposite on different sides of the world. In Australia, some people celebrate Christmas Day on the beach because it is summer!

make a sundial

What you need:

- large white paper plate
- sharp pencil or stick
- crayon

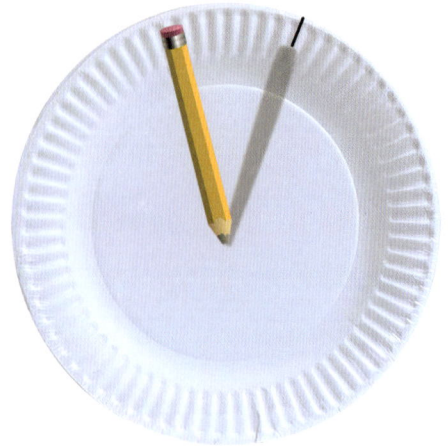

What you do:

1. Find the centre of the paper plate.

2. Put the pencil or stick in the centre so that it stands up straight.

3. Leave your sundial outside on a sunny day.

4. Check the sundial at different times of day.

5. Make a crayon mark at the end of each shadow.

What happens next: Draw pictures of the shadow.

morning 	afternoon

Geography

seven continents

The planet we live on, planet Earth, is a huge sphere. We divide it into seven **continents** and five **oceans**.

> North America   South America   Africa
> Europe   Asia   Antarctica   Australia

> Atlantic Ocean   Pacific Ocean   Indian Ocean
> Arctic Ocean   Southern (Antarctic) Ocean

Study the map on this page, and cut out the labels on page 387. Then complete the map on the following page by sticking the labels for the continents and oceans in the correct place.

spotlight on: the United Kingdom

England, Scotland, and Wales make up Great Britain. Along with Northern Ireland they are known as the United Kingdom.

Trace the capital cities and colour in the flags to complete the fact files.

SCOTLAND

NORTHERN IRELAND

IRELAND

WALES

ENGLAND

The Union Jack – the flag of the UK

England

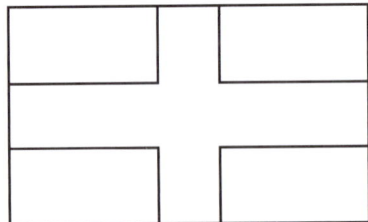

Capital city:
London

Cambridge

Wales

Capital city:
Cardiff

Brecon Beacons

London ●

Cardiff ●

Do you live in the UK? If so, find where you live on the map and mark it with a star sticker.

Scotland

Capital city:
Edinburgh

Edinburgh •

Belfast •

Highlands

Northern Ireland

Capital city:
Belfast

Dunluce Castle

Join each picture or symbol to the country it is from.

Edinburgh Castle   **Snowdonia**   **Giant's Causeway**   **Buckingham Palace**

Wales   **Scotland**   **England**   **N Ireland**

spotlight on:
Australia

Australia is a very large island and is both a country and a continent!

Trace the capital city and colour in the flag to complete the fact file.

Capital city:
Canberra

Sydney Opera House

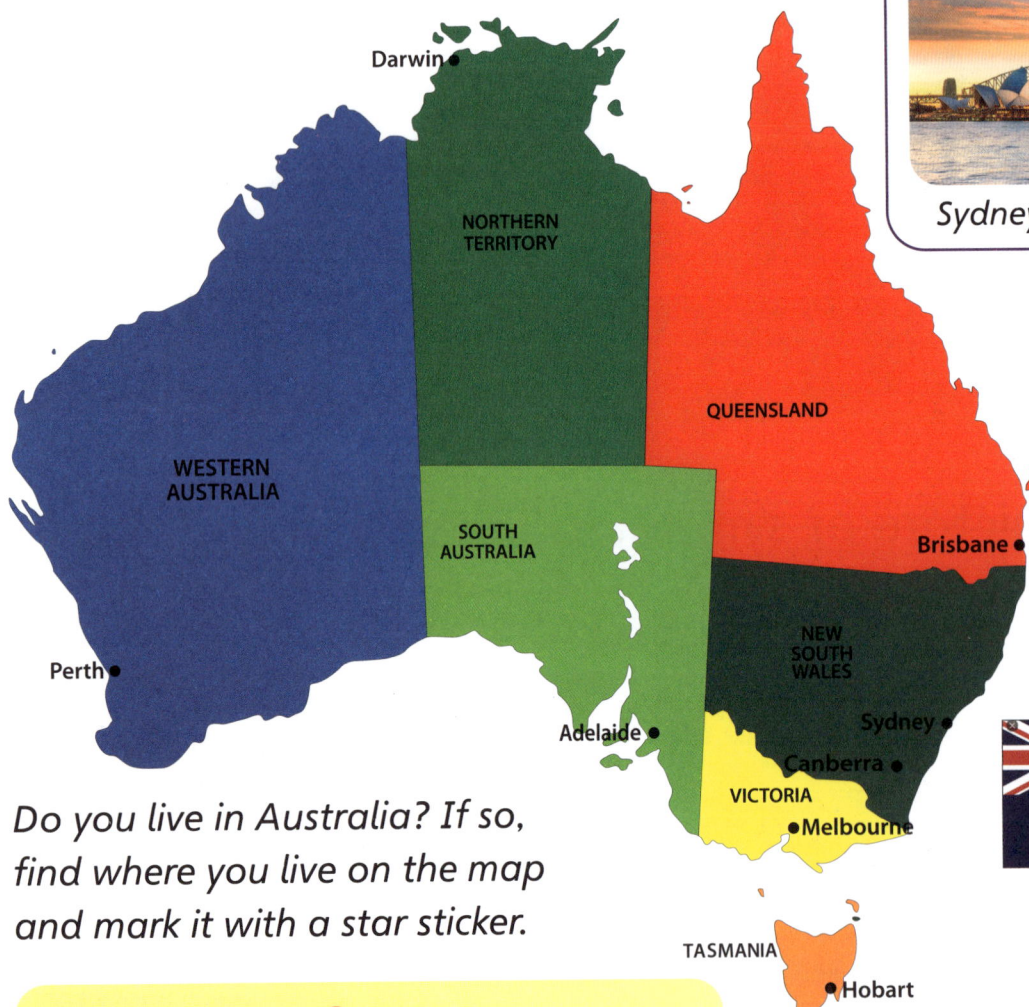

Darwin

NORTHERN
TERRITORY

QUEENSLAND

WESTERN
AUSTRALIA

SOUTH
AUSTRALIA

Brisbane

NEW
SOUTH
WALES

Perth

Adelaide

Sydney

Canberra

VICTORIA

Melbourne

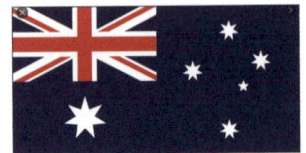

Do you live in Australia? If so, find where you live on the map and mark it with a star sticker.

TASMANIA

Hobart

Did you know?
One of the most famous rocks in the world is in Australia. It is known as **Uluru**. This gigantic sandstone rock was formed over 600 million years ago! It is 348m high and stretches over 2 miles long and 1 mile wide.

Australia has some very unusual animals that are not found anywhere else in the world. Circle the animals that come from Australia.

duck-billed platypus

zebra

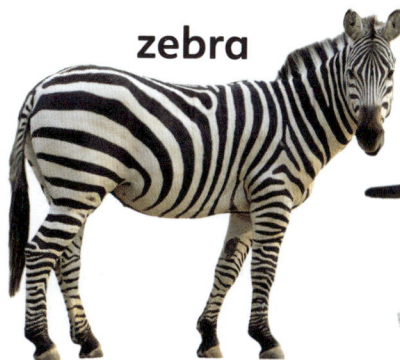

wallaby

tiger

koala

giant panda

kangaroo

polar bear

Colour in Australia on the map.

across the world

Read the two fact files, and fill in the missing words. Then answer the questions at the bottom of each page. Read both files before answering them.

Perth, Australia

animal

warm

city

Perth is the capital _____ of Western Australia. Over 2 million people live and work there in houses, flats and offices.

Perth is on flat, rolling land, near the coast. It is _____ most of the year, with hot, dry summers and cool, wet winters.

An _____ found in the area is the quokka, a short-tailed wallaby.

Which country is Castle Combe in?

Which country is Perth in?

Which place is famous for its historic buildings?

wet

village

old

Castle Combe, England

Castle Combe is a small _____ in a hilly region in the southwest of England. It is home to a few hundred people.

It is a pretty, historic village which used to hold a weekly market and a sheep fair. The houses and buildings are very _____, and many tourists visit each year.

The climate is mild and _____, with cold winters and warmer summers.

Circle **true** or **false** for each statement.

More people live in Perth than in Castle Combe.

true   false

Perth is very hilly.

true   false

The quokka is found in Castle Combe.

true   false

make your own fact file

Look at the fact files on the previous pages. Now design one of your own, for the place where *you* live. Write about how big it is, what the weather is like, and any other interesting things about it. Draw a picture of it too!

weather around the world

! The **Equator** is an invisible line that lies halfway between the **North** and **South Poles**. The hottest places on earth are found near the Equator. The poles are always extremely **cold**.

North Pole

Equator

South Pole

Where would you find each of these places – near to the poles or near the Equator?

Complete the sentences below.

The hottest places are found near the

The Equator is halfway between the North Pole and the

In the UK, the weather changes according to the time of year. The year is divided into four seasons.

The symbols below show different types of weather.
Write a label for each of the symbols.

rainy   snowy   cloudy   sunny   windy   stormy

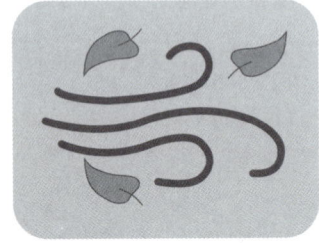

Design your own weather symbols. Label them.

Did you know?
Weather predictions help keep people safe. Correct predictions help us to plan for storms and flooding.

Draw lines to match the UK weather with the season.

spring   summer   autumn   winter

Keep a weather diary for a week. Use symbols.

Monday	Tuesday	Wednesday	Thursday

Friday	Saturday	Sunday

Write one thing that you might do in each season based on the weather.

spring ....

summer ....

autumn ....

winter ....

our world

Cut out the pictures on page 385. Which features are **human** (man-made), and which are **physical** (natural)? Stick them in the correct box below.

human

physical

Name one feature that you can see on each photo below. Is it human or physical?

FEATURE	HUMAN OR PHYSICAL

dam | river | factory | bridge | valley | coast

Find your own local features and draw them below. Choose one **human** feature and one **physical**.

Describe each place below.

Say which place you would prefer to live in and why.

finding the way

Look at the map below. Then answer the questions on the next page.

cafe

PICKWICK STREET

PRIORY STREET

ROSE AVENUE

ice cream

VICTORIA STREET

LONG HILL

GREEN LANE

SCHOOL

FOOD

DICKENS ROAD

MOSS ROAD

Write the street name for each place.

school

zoo

cafe

Imagine you are standing on Moss Road. Walk up Moss Road. Turn right onto Dickens Road. Take the first right. Which road are you on? Circle the answer.

LONG HILL   PRIORY STREET   GREEN LANE

Draw a map of where *you* live.

treasure map

Look at the map below. Then follow the clues to find where the treasure is hidden. Find the treasure chest sticker at the back of this book, and place it where the treasure is hidden.

☠ Find the ruins in the south of the island, due east of Little Bay. Start your journey there.

☠ Travel north till you meet a range of mountains.

☠ Turn westwards, and journey until you reach the fiery volcano.

☠ Next, travel north again, until you reach a large rock, shaped in the form of a human skull.

☠ Continue northwards until you reach another range of mountains.

☠ Now turn due west, and journey across the sea until you reach an island.

☠ You will find the treasure at the base of an ancient pine tree, in the very centre of the island.

Did you know?
The skull and crossbones flag at the top of a pirate ship is called a Jolly Roger.

'Due east' simply means directly east.

Draw your own treasure map.

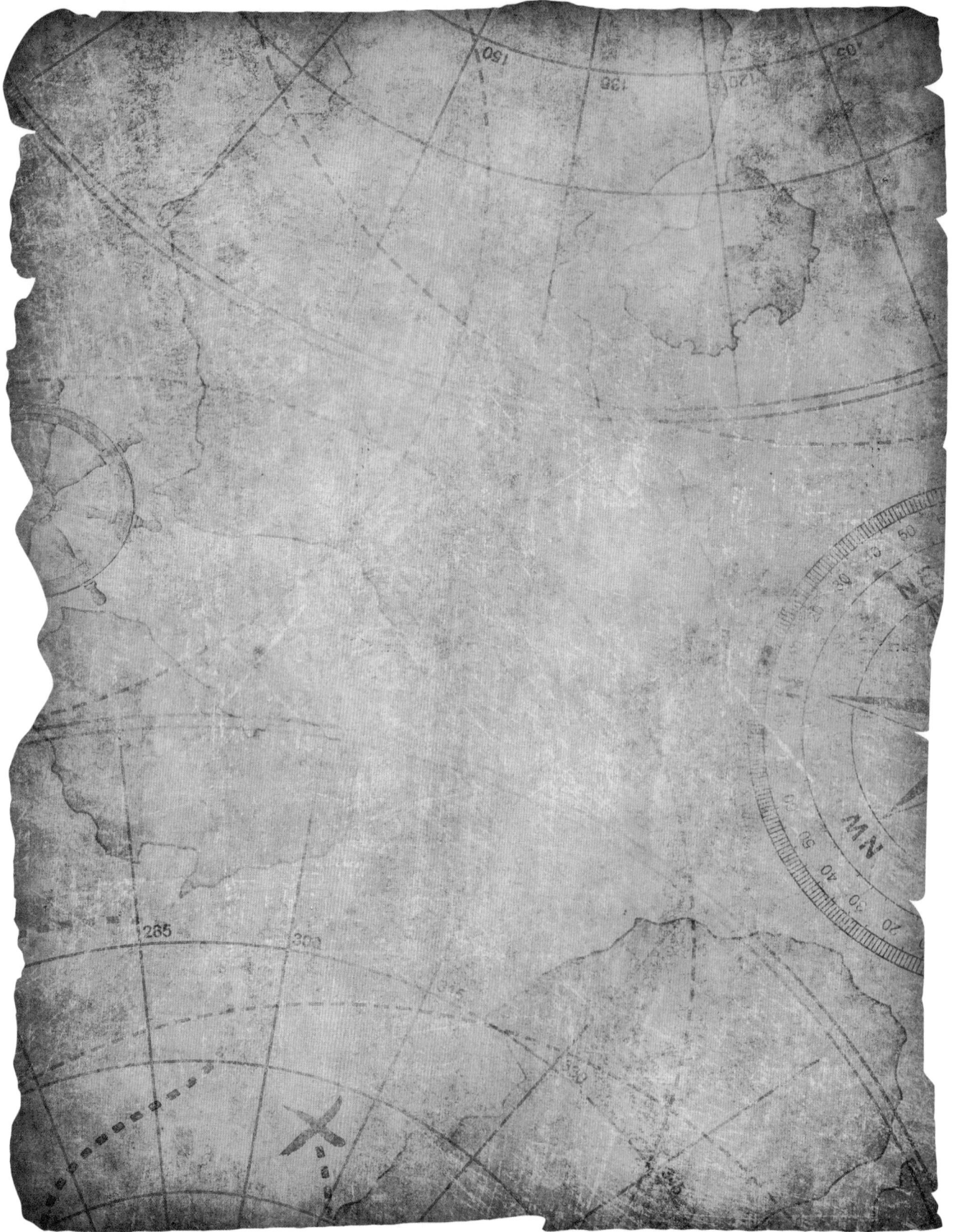

History

now and then

Colour in the correct clock for each description.

	past	present	future
something that is **happening now**			
something that **happened before now**			
something that **hasn't happened yet**			

Do each of these forms of transport belong to the **past** or the **present**? Circle **past** in green, and **present** in red. Then join up the **old** and **current** versions.

As new things are invented, daily life changes. Look at each of the pairs of objects below, and say how you think the new invention changed people's lives.

Place these phones in order of when you think they were made, starting with the **oldest** [1] through to the **most recent** [4].

Toys are one of the things that have changed over the years. Cut out the toys on page 387 and place them in one of the boxes below according to whether you think they are **old** or **new**.

Old Toys

New Toys

Choose one of the old toys and one of the new toys to compare. Draw them below.

wooden   tin   electronic   plastic   handmade
simple   metal   mass-produced   colourful

Using some of the words above, describe some of the differences and similarities between the old toy and the new toy.

Which is your favourite toy? Why?

Did you know?
Until the 1960s, toy soldiers were made out of lead, which is poisonous! Nowadays, toys have to pass strict safety checks.

spotlight on the past:
The Gunpowder Plot

The Gunpowder Plot was a plan to blow up the Houses of Parliament in London and kill the king.

In 1605, James I was King of England. Catholics were very unhappy with the way that he treated them. A group of conspirators (plotters), led by a man called Robert Catesby, and including Guy Fawkes, rented a cellar below the Houses of Parliament – where the government meets to discuss politics – and filled it with gunpowder which they planned to explode during the state opening of Parliament on November 5, 1605.

Guido Fawkes   Robert Catesby

However, the plot was discovered, and Guy Fawkes was caught red-handed in the cellar. The other conspirators were caught a few days later. They were all executed.

Every year on the anniversary of the plot, people in the United Kingdom celebrate the fact that the plot failed. It is known as Guy Fawkes Night, or Bonfire Night. The celebrations include bonfires and fireworks.

James I was Protestant. The plotters were Catholic. Both these religions are Christian, but they had big differences and conflicts.

Read the text carefully. Use the information to solve the clues and complete the crossword below.

CLUES

ACROSS

I. Another word for plotters.

DOWN

I. They hid the barrels here.

2. An explosive powder used in guns.

3. Another word for 'blow up'.

4. The name of the king.

5. Something we light on 5th November each year.

GUNPOWDER

CONSPIRATORS

JAMES

CELLAR

EXPLODE

BONFIRE

Put these events in order from **first** [1] to **last** [4].

The plot was foiled and the plotters were put to death.

Each year, people in the UK celebrate Guy Fawkes Night with fireworks and bonfires.

James I was King of England. He treated Catholics unfairly.

Guy Fawkes and some other Catholics plotted to kill the king.

If you could speak to Guy Fawkes, what questions would you ask him?

Do you celebrate Bonfire Night? What do you do? Do you celebrate any other occasions with bonfires or fireworks? Write about it below.

Design your own fireworks!

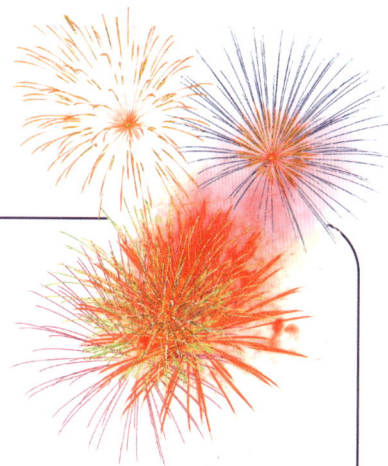

history near you

Write about an event that happened where you lived – something that changed the place. It might have happened long ago, or it could be more recent.

What happened?	When did it happen?

What changed?

Draw a picture of what happened, or what changed.

explorers through time

On the next few pages are profiles of some famous explorers.

Christopher Columbus – or 'the man who discovered America' – was born in Genoa, Italy, in 1451.

He wanted to find a westward sea passage to India and China. He found backing for his plan from the Spanish king and queen who gave him money. His fleet of three ships set sail across the Atlantic. In October 1492, land was sighted. Columbus believed he had reached the Indies: in fact, he had reached what we know call the Bahamas.

His discovery of the New World changed the course of world history.

What happened first? Put the following sentences in the correct order from **first** [1] to **last** [4].

The Spanish king and queen backed his voyage	Columbus was born in Italy	Columbus landed in the New World	Columbus set sail with three ships

What things would you put in your backpack if you were going on a sea adventure?

Columbus was a great explorer, but he and his men treated the local people badly. Some see him as the father of the slave trade.

HISTORY

345

What do you think it would have been like to travel in one of Columbus's ships? What is travelling by ship like today? Write some of the differences.

Amelia Earhart was born in Kansas, America in 1897. She was a tomboy growing up, but only became interested in planes when visiting an air show with her father in 1920.

She went on her first plane flight that day, and fell in love with flying. She broke many records, most famously becoming the first woman to fly solo across the Atlantic Ocean. She hoped to land in Paris, but bad weather caused her to land in a cow field in Ireland!

Attempting to fly around the world, her plane disappeared over the Pacific Ocean, and neither she, nor her plane, were ever found.

What things would you put in your backpack if you were going on a plane journey?

What do you think it would have been like to fly in Amelia Earhart's time? What is travelling by plane like today? Write some of the differences.

Have you ever made a journey by plane? What was it like? Where did you set off from, and where did you go to? Write about it below, and mark the places on the map.

Neil Armstrong was born in Ohio, America in 1930. He earned his pilot's licence at 16, and when he was older he was a fighter pilot during the Korean War, then later a test pilot, flying experimental planes.

In 1962, Armstrong was selected for the NASA Astronaut Corps, and in 1969 he commanded the Apollo 11 on its space mission, successfully landing the lunar module on the Moon. After landing, Armstrong was the first to leave the craft and walk on the Moon, famously saying, "That's one small step for man, one giant leap for mankind".

He and his fellow astronauts, Buzz Aldrin and Michael Collins, safely returned to Earth as heroes.

Would you like to travel in space? Why/why not?

What things would you put in your backpack if you were going on a space voyage?

Did you know?
From Earth, both the Sun and the Moon look about same size. This is because the Moon is 400 times smaller than the Sun, but also 400 times closer to Earth!

How do you think space travel will change in the future?

Astronaut making repairs to the ISS (International Space Station).

Read the fact files on each explorer, then match the clues and the pictures to the explorer.

I learned to fly at the age of 16.

I was the first woman to fly across the Atlantic.

I was born in Genoa, in 1451.

Amelia Earhart

Neil Armstrong

Christopher Columbus

close to home

Write about a famous person who is from where you live. What did they do? How did they shape history? Did they change your local area?

Name:

Date of birth:

Date of death:

Where they are from:

Draw a picture of them here:

What are they famous for?

An interesting fact about them:

Hands-on

same grapheme, different sound ✂--

Cut out these words for the activity on page 35.

denied	chief	shriek	spies
field	tried	fried	movie
replied	priest	belief	untie

what happens next? ✂--

Cut out these sentences for the activity on page 109.

Mum gave Tom a sparkler.

Tom and Elsie went to the village bonfire.

She told him to _____

It was Bonfire Night.

Mum gave the children some hard-boiled eggs.

Tomorrow they would _____

Sonia, Hugo and Edie painted the eggs.

It was Easter.

bumblebee craft

Cut out the pieces below to make your own busy bumblebee. Glue them together, then attach to a lollipop stick, or cut out the black band (a) below and roll and glue it into a ring, which can be glued to the bumblebee, so that it can be worn on your finger!

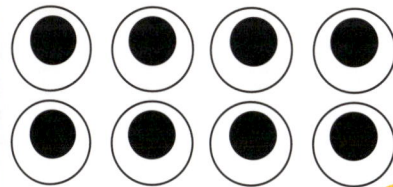
The eyes will be fiddly to cut out, so there are a couple of spare sets!

a

all in order ✂----

Cut out these numbers for the activity on page 151.

6	19	5	16	4
3	1	15	7	18
11	8	20	10	14
9	12	17	2	13

weighty business ✂----

Cut out these cards for the activity on page 224.

place value bingo ✂ ---

Cut out these cards for the activity on page 168.

	1 ten **8 ones**		**3 tens** **3 ones**
	2 tens **1 one**		**3 tens** **5 ones**
	2 tens **2 ones**		**3 tens** **7 ones**
	2 tens **6 ones**		**4 tens** **1 one**
	2 tens **9 ones**		**4 tens** **3 ones**
	3 tens **0 ones**		**5 tens** **0 ones**

ordinal numbers ✂ - - -

Cut out these cards for the activity on page 174.

9th Monkey	11th Dog	3rd Tiger
4th Rabbit	2nd Ox	6th Snake
8th Goat	7th Horse	12th Pig
1st Rat	5th Dragon	10th Rooster

number pairs ✂---

Cut out these cards for the activity on page 200.

HANDS ON

18 – 13	9 – 3	16 – 9	12 – 3
2 + 3	4 + 2	1 + 6	5 + 4
17 – 6	8 – 0	20 – 3	10 – 6
6 + 5	4 + 4	9 + 8	4 + 0
20 – 10	15 – 3	18 – 15	16 – 3
7 + 3	9 + 3	1 + 2	8 + 5

number pairs

363

my calendar ✂----

Cut out the labels below to use for the activity on page 238.

1	2	3	4	5	6
7	8	9	10	11	
12	13	14	15		
16	17	18	19		
20	21	22	23		
24	25	26	27		
28	29	30	31		

Saturday

Monday Tuesday
Wednesday Friday
Thursday Sunday

January July

February August

March September

April October

May November

June December

bingo cards ✂--

Cut out the clocks below to use for the activity on page 244.

days of the week ✂----

Cut out these cards for the activity on page 236.

Saturday	Friday	Tuesday
Sunday	Wednesday	Thursday	Monday

money matters ✂----

Cut out the coins below to use for the activity on page 245.

shape patterns ✂----

Cut out the shapes below to use for the activity on page 259.

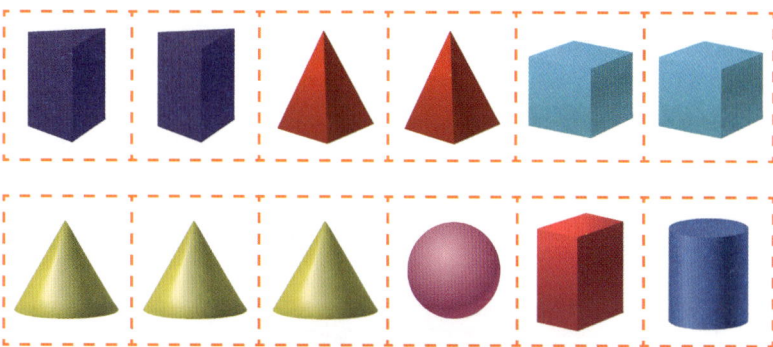

3D shapes

Cut out these shapes for the activity on page 254.

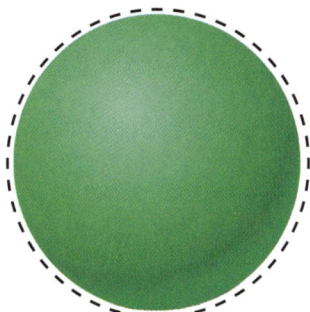

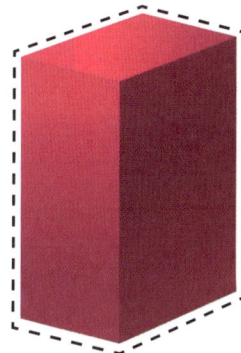

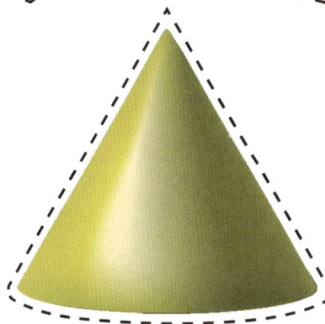

plant habitats

Cut out these cards for the activity on page 271.

shapes around us

Cut out the images below to use for the activity on pages 256-257.

monster turns ✂---

Cut out these cards for the activity on page 264.

the human body ✂---

Cut out the labels below to use for the activity on page 292.

| head | hair | ears | eyes | mouth | nose | teeth | fingers |

| shoulder | leg | knee | elbow | arm | foot | toes | hand |

who's who ✂---

Cut out the animals below and on the next page to use for the activity on pages 284-285.

magpie

leopard

lizard

goldfish

rooster

chameleon

crocodile

shark

hamster

frog

turtle

tuna

deer

salamander

penguin

measuring ✂---

Cut out this ruler to use for the activites on pages 221 and 222.

our world ✂ ----

Cut out the pictures below to use for the activity on page 326.

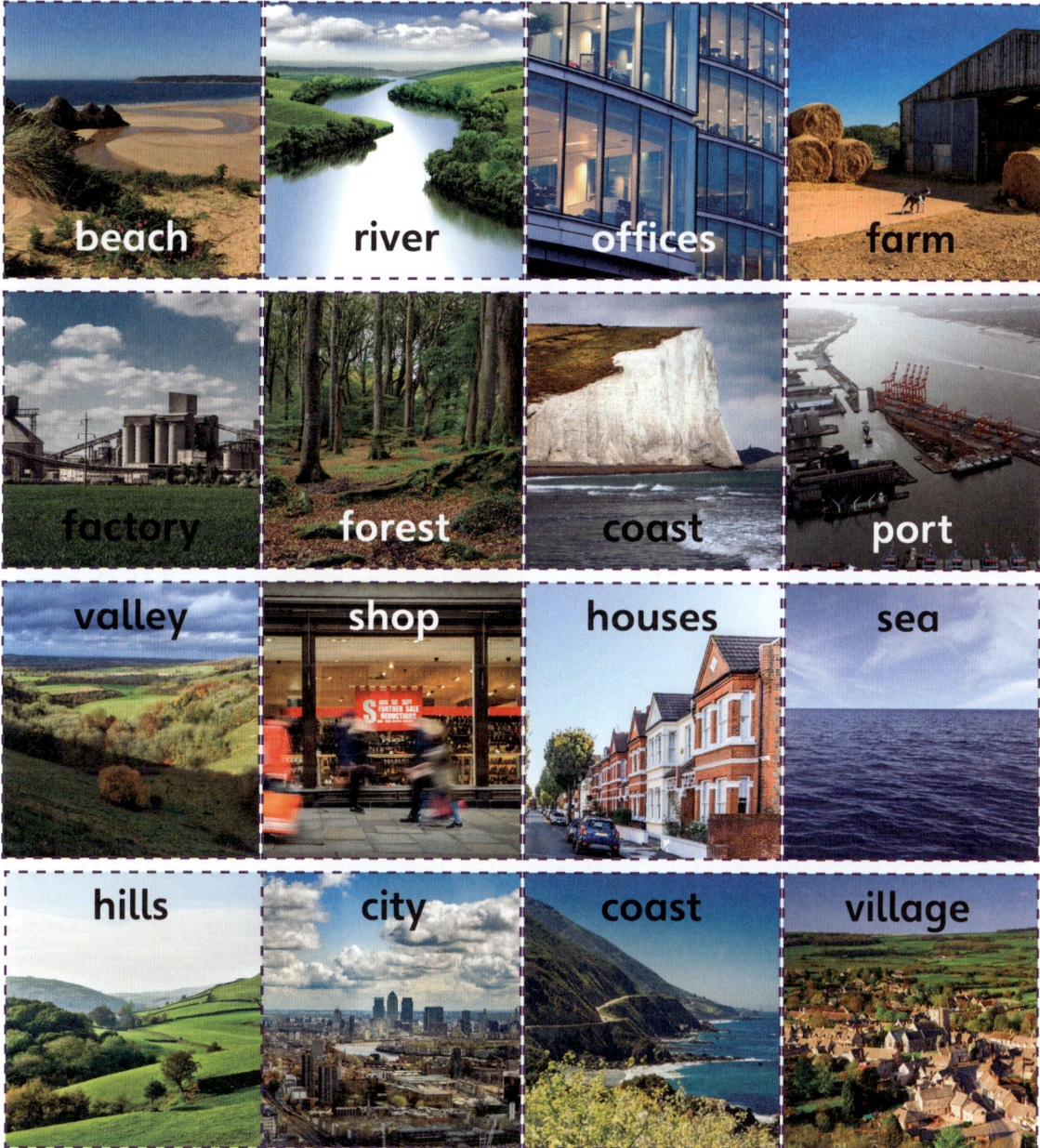

beach	river	offices	farm
factory	forest	coast	port
valley	shop	houses	sea
hills	city	coast	village

continents and oceans ✂--

Cut out the labels below to use for the activity on page 315.

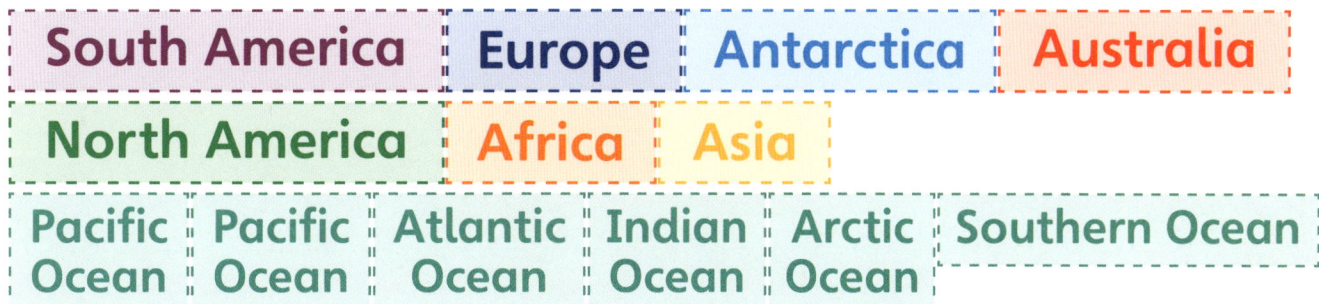

| South America | Europe | Antarctica | Australia |

| North America | Africa | Asia |

| Pacific Ocean | Pacific Ocean | Atlantic Ocean | Indian Ocean | Arctic Ocean | Southern Ocean |

now and then ✂--

Cut out the toys below to use for the activity on page 338.

A Book
About Me

Draw your favourite thing to do.

I like to eat _____

Draw your favourite food.

My name is

_____ •

Draw a picture of yourself.

My favourite colour is

_____ •

Draw a picture of something in your favourite colour.

I am ____ years old.

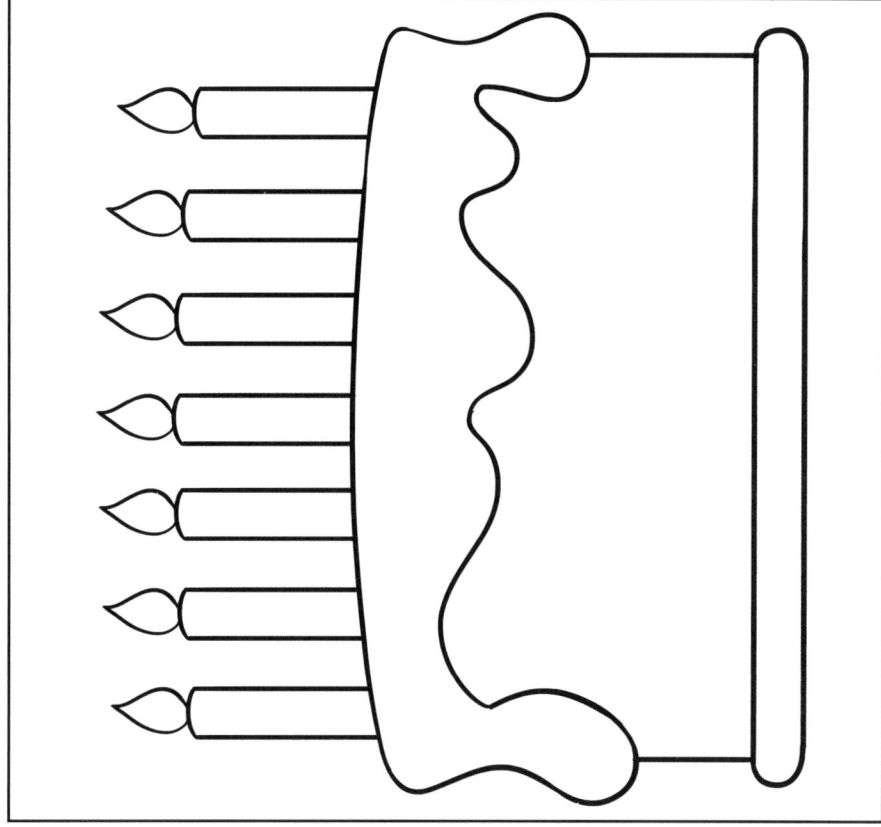

Colour the candles to show how many years old you are.

When I grow up, I want to ____.

Draw a picture of what you want to do when you grow up.

This is my family.

Draw a picture of your family.

I live in _____

Draw a picture of your home.

Answers

Phonics Section

page 28

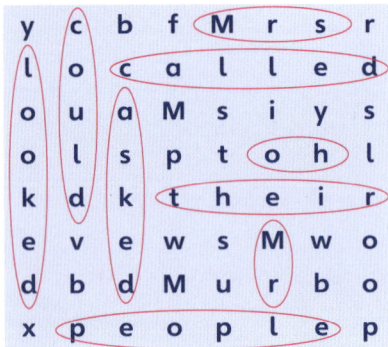

page 44

chips, shade, prowl

page 50

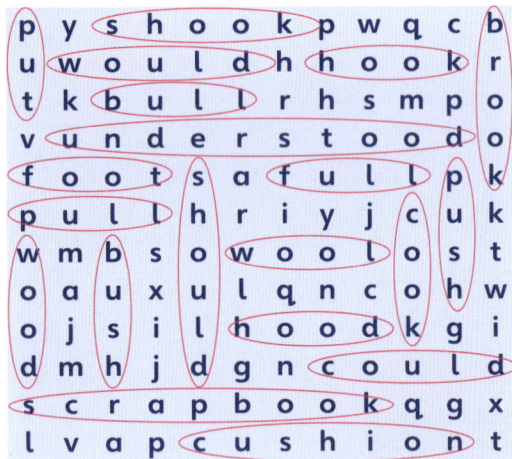

page 58

home and row, leaf and tree, horse and ball, chair and bear

page 59

bird and Earth, cake and rain, shoe and zoo, bike and fly, flowers and mouse

page 65

knight, knife, knee, gnome, knot, sign

page 72

jump	drink	tent	parnt	dress	frog	crab	smole	bell	link	ring
sink	wrote	design	melt	brant	little	choop	crept	wrinkle	gnarl	spill
knee	gnome	photo	knife	said	loof	asked	knight	wheel	gnat	kneel
knit	when	knuckle	knock	reign	moob	sign	gnaw	wrist	dolphin	wring
lamp	knob	knead	signed	know	ranp	wrap	knot	wreath	write	shelf
bulb	swing	chat	unwrap	wreck	boam	wren	wrong	milk	belt	swim
chin	even	tune	cane	these	menk	rose	chase	slope	rule	flat
frame	spade	theme	kite	home	choaw	hide	skate	smile	slide	chime
cube	grape	treasure	flame	bike	frime	swede	stripe	decision	globe	cute
pillow	broke	nose	role	tape	santy	lane	hope	came	stile	chimp
fish	wig	plane	lute	blink	plime	shed	stale	ride	slap	plot

the picture is of a butterfly

Writing and Reading Sections

page 78

boat, lion, hippo, train, slide, apple, horse, chair, bread

page 79

armchair, ladybird, buttercup, moonlight, postbox, basketball

page 83

glasses, stitches, dishes, walruses, bunches, dresses, peaches, boxes, watches

page 84

toothbrushes, clocks, crosses, hats, guitars, foxes, cakes, sandwiches, fortresses, kittens, hutches

page 89

can't; we'll, wasn't, I'll, they're

page 93

7; Saturday and Sunday

page 94

I like to play tennis with Sam. / The beach was very busy on Sunday. / My sister and I both have dark hair. / When it is cold I wear gloves and a hat. / The postman came to the door. The dog barked angrily. / The party on Saturday was fun. We played lots of games.

page 95

I like going to the circus. / Would you like to come, too? / When does it start? / The circus tent is very big. / The clowns are hilarious! / Would you like a snack? / How does the acrobat do that? We saw a lion. / I enjoyed it very much!

page 96

Dad fixed the toy. / My blocks fell down. / Can you guess who it is? / Chocolate cake is yummy! / The glass of water is cold! / Katie loves to read.

page 98-101

fish → leaves / flew → pulled / biscuit → snowball / caterpillars → strawberries / swam → ran / cake → plant / mud → water / bed → curtains / wash → ride / alligator → dog / apple → trainer / tree → wall / bath → water / pumpkin → ball / river → road / drove → skied

/ table → swing / pigeon → fish / sand → snow / frog → salad / threw → read / ceiling → floor / smashed → washed

page 109
It was Bonfire Night. Tom and Elsie went to the village bonfire. Mum gave Tom a sparkler. She told him to … ; It was Easter. Mum gave the children some eggs. Sonia, Hugo and Edie painted the eggs. Tomorrow they would …

page 112
2, 5, 1, 3, 4

page 113
[1] Amy got her lunch . . . [2] Amy didn't know . . . [3] Amy dropped her food . . .

page 125-126
Lion / Mouse / Mouse ran over his tail / He thought Lion would eat him / He stepped in a hunters' net / He chewed through the rope. Message: Everyone can be helpful …

page 128
mouse, walk, sleep, me (the owner)

page 129
bright, tonight and might / sight, fright, knight, white, bite, etc / 'I wish I' is repeated. /

'may' does not have a rhyming word.

page 131
books / the school library / after school on Monday

page 133
nectar and pollen / the bumblebee / pollen

page 134
Ben / Sue / the yellow hat with spots

page 135
They are both going to play football / Lin is playing with a friend, Jen is playing with a team

page 136-137
information / no / all three / helping a person

page 139
ploughing and carrying goods / a foal / draft horse / miniature horse / saddle horse

page 141
summer / autumn / spring

page 143
paper and a pencil / O and X / get three of the same shape in a row

page 144
1, 4, 5, 3, 2

Numbers and Arithmetic Sections

page 151
a) 5, b) 9, c) 20, d) 13, e) 10, f) 11

page 153

1	2	3					8	9	10
11	12	13					18	19	20
21									30
31	32	33	34	35	36	37	38	39	40
41	42	43		45	46		48	49	50
51	52	53	54	55	56	57	58	59	60
61	62	63	64	65					70
71	72	73	74	75	76	77	78	79	80
81	82	83		85	86		88	89	90
91	92	93	94			97	98	99	100

a snowman

page 156
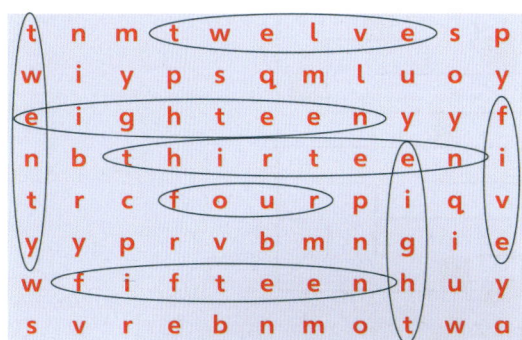

1 a) 18, b) 13, c) 20, d) 8
2 a) 15, b) 5, c) 12, d) 4

page 159

22	43	55	70	100
75	80	24	90	99	88
21	77	53	12	80	60
90	15	10	70	33	34
33	26	78	60	21	22
88	36	50	20	54	55
46	40	25	60	32	78
21	22	30	46	47	20
	19	20	8	9	10
	6	12	10	30	63
	0	2	40	44

page 161-2
1) 12, 16; 2) 30, 50; 3) 50, 30; 4) 40, 70; 5) 8, 16; 6) 25, 15

page 163
a) 25, b) 16, c) 18, d) 13, e) 11, f) 27, g) 30, h) 19, i) 24, j) 21, k) 14

page 164
16; 7; 9; 2

page 165
1) 8, even, 2) 9, odd

page 166
1) 2 tens, 4 ones = 24; 2) 3 tens, 6 ones = 36; 3) 5 tens, 1 one = 51; 4) 4 tens, 7 ones = 47

page 167
27; 35; 16; 28; 50; 47; 43; 82
SCHOOL BUZZ

page 169
37—30—7; 29—20—9; 92—90—2; 65—60—5 ;
23—20—3; 48—40—8; 76—70—6; 54—50—4

page 170
a) 21 > 12; b) 38 < 43; c) 12 < 43; d) 33 < 38;
e) 21 = 21; f) 43 > 33

page 173
47 < 69; 88 > 59; 33 > 27; 73 < 91; 64 > 48;
85 < 91

page 175
Rat; Pig; 6th; 9th; Horse; Ox

page 176-178
1) 16, 28; 2) 4, 2; 3) 11, 8;
4) 14, 10; 5) 18, 15; 6) 3, 21;
7) 14, 6; 8) 20, 10; 9) 18, 12

page 180
15; 5; 6; 5; 7; 20

page 181
Ginger 3+2+2=7; Luna 2+4+2=8;
Sooty 2+1+2=5; Smokey 5+4+1=10
Smokey has the most wool

page 182
a) 18; b) ⬚ c) 9; d)

e)

f)   g) 16; h)   i) 30

page 183
1+5=6; 5+1=6; 2+3=5; 3+2=5;
4+7=11; 7+4=11; 7+8=15; 8+7=15
add

page 184
<; =; >
<; <; =; >; >

page 185
a) 9; b) 15; c) 14; d) 14; e) 16; f) 20
g) 8; h) 6; i) 5; j) 0; k) 4; l) 5

page 186-7
6+8=14; 8+7=15; 5+7=12;
9+9=18; 7+6=13; 6+9=15

page 188
13; 15; 14; 18; 19; 16; 12; 17

THE BIRD SEED

page 189

page 190
14; 6; 10; 9; 6; 10

page 191
a) 2; b) 14; c)

d)   e)

f) 6; g)   h) 11

page 192
6; 9; 10; 4

page 193
5 (I); 4 (G); 1 (S); 9 (W); 2 (L);
3 (H); 6 C); 7 (O); 0 (A); 8 (N)
WHO IS CALLING?

page 194
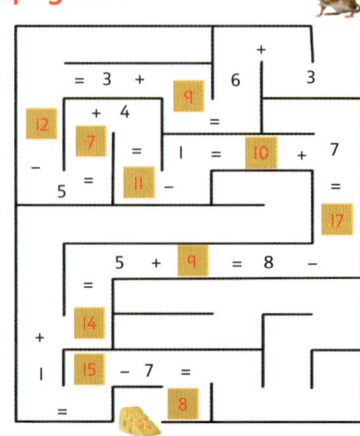

The mouse 8 the 🧀 !

page 195
6-3=3; 4+4=8; 2+5=7; 8-7=1

page 196

page 197
3, 3; 5, 5; 3, 3; 2, 2

page 198
20—12—8; 20—11—9; 20—10—10; 20—19—1;
20—7—13; 20—5—15; 20—14—6; 20—20—0;
20—17—3;20—9—11; 20—18—2; 20—16—4

page 199
3+5=8, 5+3=8, 8-3=5, 8-5=3;
3+2=5, 2+3=5, 5-3=2, 5-2=3;
4+3=7, 3+4=7, 7-4=3, 7-3=4

page 200
a) 11; b) 7; c) 16; d) 4; e) 8; f) 3; g) 8; h) 9;
i) 11; j) 5

page 201-2
1a) 10, b) 10, c) 10; 2a) 6, b) 6, c) 6;
3a) 9, b) 9, c) 9; 4a) 4, b) 4, c) 4
5a) 11, b) 11, c) 11; 6a) 12, b) 12, c) 12;
7a) 15, b) 15, c) 15; 8a) 17, b) 17, c) 17

page 203
3; 13-9=4; 16-9=7; 17-9=8

page 204
8; 14; 10; 4; 20; 16; 12; 18; 6

page 205
5; 4; 6; 9; 10; 8

page 206
14; 8

page 207
5 sets of 2; 5x2=10; 2+2=4; 2x2=4;
6 sets of 2; 6x2=12; 2+2+2+2=8 4x2=8;
6x2=12, 2x6=12; 5x2=10, 2x5=10;
4x2=8, 2x4=8

page 208-9
1) 5+5+5+5+5+5=30, 6 sets of 6, 6x5=30;
2) 8x5=40;
3) 5x2=10, 2x5=10; 4) 5x3=15, 3x5=15;
5) 5x4=20, 4x5=20
6) 5x10=50; 7) 9x10=90; 8) 10x3=30,
3x10=30; 9) 10x5=50, 5x10=50

page 210

page 211-2
1) 2; 2) 14, 3) 3; 4) 2; 5) 12; 6) 8; 7) 3

page 213

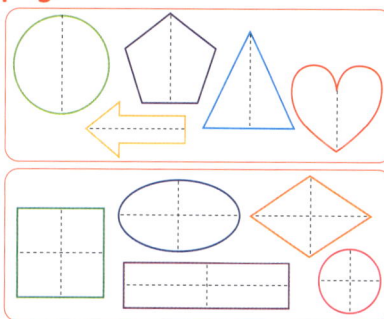

page 214
a) yes, no, yes; b) no, no, yes;
c) the group of 2 children

Measurement and Geometry Sections

page 218
white; Gerald

page 219
Casey (longest), Chloe (shortest);
Callan and Craig; Chloe; Casey

page 220
D; B, 7; D; A

page 223
black; 3cm; pink and orange

page 224
robin, cat, dog, tiger, elephant

page 225
robin; tiger;
[1] cotton wool, [2] wool, [3] shoes,
[4] backpack, [5] table, [6] sofa

page 228
glass F, glass D, glass B

page 230
500ml, 300ml, 150ml, 200ml, 425ml, 75ml

page 235

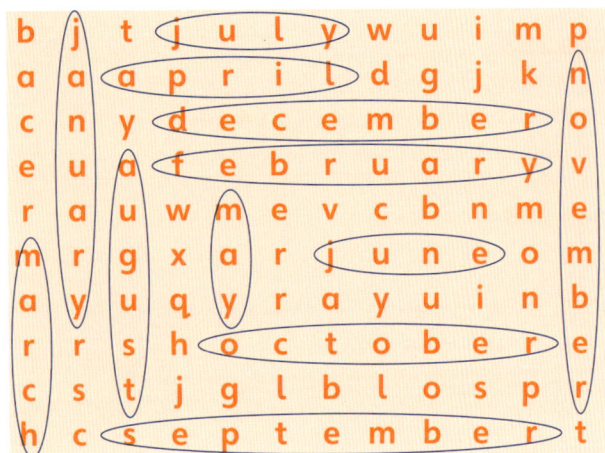

November, June, April and August, April

page 236

Tuesday and Thursday, Saturday

page 241

half past three [3.30], ten o'clock [10.00],
half past four [4.30], seven o'clock [7.00],
half past one [1.30], half past nine [9.30]

page 243

half past eight [8.30], half past one [1.30],
six o'clock [6.00], half past ten [10.30]

page 245

page 246

Alonso 10p, Gina 5p, Ahmed 20p,
Aisha 12p, Zach 15p, Becky 18p

page 249-250

1) 6; 2) £3; 3) 10p; 4) 2, 4;
5) £2; 6) 50p, 40p; 7) ball; 8) £4, £1

page 253

8 circles, 8 triangles, 13 rectangles;
rectangle

page 255

page 259

page 261

right, left, right

page 263

Sam, May

page 265

apple, banana, pear, grapes;
move forwards 2 squares

page 266

2, right, 3, left, 1

Science Section

page 268

roots; leaves; trunk; branches; crown

page 283

fish [10], amphibians [6]

page 290

1) leg, foot; 2) foot; 3) fin, tail; 4) leg, foot;
5) tail, eye

page 300

1) The key because it is not flexible;

2) The jug because it is not transparent;
3) The towel because it is not hard;
4) The teabag because it is not waterproof

page 309

1) blossom, warmer, lambs; 2) ice cream,
beach, days; 3) leaves, colder, bonfires;
4) gloves, snowmen, cocoa

page 310-311

from east to west; directly overhead; summer;
shorter

Geography and History Sections

page 320-321

England; Australia; Castle Combe;
true; false; false

page 323

Equator; South Pole

page 327

river–physical; factory–human; valley–physical;
dam–human; bridge–human; coast–physical

page 331

Dickens Road, Long Hill, Priory Street; Green Ln

page 337

2, 4, 3, 1

page 341

Across: 1) conspirators. Down: 1) cellar, 2)
gunpowder, 3) explode, 4) James, 5) bonfire

page 342

1) James I was King ... 2) Guy Fawkes ...
3) The plot was foiled ... 4) Each year ...

page 345

2, 1, 4, 3

Wonders of Learning

Well done!

You have

COMPLETED

this

WORKBOOK

CERTIFICATE

Congratulations to:

....

(name)

for completing this **Wonders of Learning** workbook.

You are a learning star!

What was your favourite part of the book?

What do you want to learn about next?

....
(parent/helper)

....
(date)

A	A	B	B	C	C	D	D	E	E
F	F	G	G	H	H	I	I	J	J
K	K	L	L	M	M	N	N	O	O
P	P	Q	Q	R	R	S	S	T	T
U	U	V	V	W	W	X	X	Y	Y
Z	Z	a	a	a	a	b	b	b	c
c	c	d	d	d	e	e	e	e	e
f	f	f	g	g	g	h	h	i	i
i	i	j	j	j	k	k	k	l	l
l	m	m	m	n	n	n	o	o	o
o	p	p	p	q	q	r	r	r	s
s	s	t	t	t	u	u	u	v	v
w	w	w	x	x	y	y	y	z	z